# The Porter Process:

## 5 steps to unlock your child's potential from K to career

# Dr. Patricia Porter

## Limits of Liability and Disclaimer of Warranty

The author and publisher shall not be liable for your misuse of this material. This book is strictly for informational and educational purposes.

## Warning – Disclaimer

The purpose of this book is to educate and entertain. The author and/or publisher do not guarantee that anyone following these techniques, suggestions, tips, ideas, or strategies will become successful. The author and/or publisher shall have neither liability nor responsibility to anyone with respect to any loss or damage caused, or alleged to be caused, directly or indirectly by the information contained in this book.

ISBN-13: 978-1519131706
ISBN-10: 1519131704

*To the many parents who have shared their struggles
and concerns and helped me understand
how they can change children's lives.*

# Connecting with Dr. Patricia Porter

patricia@leadingtolearning.com

(1) 604 733 0543

LinkedIn    https://ca.linkedin.com/in/drpporter

Twitter - https://twitter.com/PatriciaPorter

Facebook - https://www.facebook.com/patricia.porter.71619?fref=ts

# Contents

# Introduction

This book is for you if…
    … you are concerned about your child's education
    … you want to help your child reach his or her full learning potential
    … you are ready to make a difference in your child's learning life
    … you want to take the stress and frustration out of helping your child succeed in
      school

## Why I wrote this book

In my 30-year teaching career I have seen too many children failing to reach their learning potential because they were not getting the support they needed. I want to change this.

Our children are the future and they deserve the best we can give them. Giving children the best is not difficult. It is easy and remarkably inexpensive to make simple changes that ensure children get the kind of support that leads to school success. All it takes is a willingness to support the most influential people in children's lives – their parents.

You know and I know the best way to help children succeed in life is by helping them succeed in school. You have a vital role to play in making this happen. This book shows you how.

## My story

I am a teacher and, like many teachers, teaching is in my bones. I loved nearly every minute of my 35-year teaching career. I spent most of it working with children with learning difficulties, students who were struggling to keep up in class, were losing confidence in their abilities and had given up trying to learn. I always wondered why learning was difficult for some children and easy for others.

My 'Ah-ha' moment happened during a training course given by world experts on children's learning. What I learned changed my life and it can change yours too.

Some children learn better than other because they know how to learn. Simple isn't it? Makes a lot of sense. You need to know how to do something if you are going to do it well. The problem is we don't spend a lot of time helping children learn how to learn. Most of the time we spend teaching them what to learn. Teachers are busy trying to get through the curriculum and parents are busy helping with homework. No one is concentrating on helping children learn how to learn.

Children who don't know how to learn, who haven't developed the skills they need, who don't know the strategies that make learning easy and fun, never reach their full learning potential.

I had the answer to my question as to why learning was difficult for some children and easy for others. Now I had to work out what to do with that information.

Fortunately I was trained to diagnose which skills children lacked and how to help develop those skills. I used my training to help students in school who were struggling to learn.

For the first time I truly understood what 'to learn' meant. I understood why some children learned more quickly and easily than others. And I realized that it is you, parents, who have the power to make learning happen.

(For more details about my life and career go to www.leadingtolearning.com and read my About page.)

After working with many parents who wanted to know why their bright child was struggling to learn I realized I had a process that I could share. The Porter Process was born. This book is my attempt to write down the process that I have been using to enable children to learn.

# How to use this book

I have created a workbook that guides you through the steps that help you create your child's formula for success.

There are activities at the end of nearly every section of the book. Working through these activities will give you a better understanding of your role in helping your child succeed in school and how you can make that role work for you and your child. Read this book with a pencil in your hand and be ready to underline parts that are important to you, to make notes and to start working on the activities.

The book is in three sections.

- The first section of the book helps set the scene for the activities you will be doing. It helps you understand the special role you play in helping your child learn and why guessing what support your child needs will not lead to success. The activities at the end of each chapter will help you get ready to implement the 5-Step Porter Process.

- In the second section of the book you are gently guided through the five simple steps that are the heart of the Porter Process and that allow you to discover exactly what support your child needs and how you can provide it. As you work through each step you will be building up your child's Formula for Success.

- The third section of the book is for use as you go through the steps. Here you will find a host of practical, proven strategies you can use to help your child reach his or her full learning potential. I don't expect you to read, or use, them all, only those that are relevant to your child's specific learning needs.

# Section 1
# Education: The Missing Piece

# 1.

# Grey area students

## What you will learn

- Who are Grey Area Students

- Why there are so many students who are 'grey area' kids

- Misconceptions about these students

- The hidden cost of underachievement

- Action that can be taken to remediate this situation

- The importance of trusting your instinct

## Why this information is important

- It helps you determine whether your child is one of the students who are missing out so you can help your child get the education he or she needs.

There is something missing in most, if not all, K – 12 education systems and it is not all the fault of schools or teachers. Children are not reaching their full learning potential. As many as one out of two students are not getting the grades they are capable of getting because they are not getting the support they need to succeed.

I was a teacher for over 30 years and I know how hard teachers work and how much effort they put into helping children do well in school. Not all schools and not all teachers are perfect but on the whole they do a good job, often in difficult circumstances. Yet despite all the work teachers do and the hours they spend preparing lessons and upgrading their qualifications, many students fall through the gap between what schools provide and what support they need.

Without this support students struggle to learn, fail to get the grades they are capable of getting, and start the downward spiral to failure. They are underachievers. Under-achievement occurs when a child's performance is below what is expected based on his or her ability. I call these students, the ones who are performing below their level of ability, 'grey area' students.

Grey area students are students who are bright but who are not getting the marks that they are capable of getting and know they should be getting. Grey is a color that is easy to miss. It is a color that is inconspicuous, a background color, a color that is easy to ignore. Grey area students are just like that.

Grey area students come in many different disguises. Here are descriptions of a few that I have met during my teaching career.

* *Johnny got good grades in math but poor grades in reading and writing. He was a bright student and no one knew why his writing skills were so poor. Everyone assumed that the reason he didn't write well was because he didn't try hard enough.*

* *Sally's teacher told her parents that Sally didn't focus in class, that she lacked concentration and spent her time daydreaming. So no wonder her grades were so low!*

* *Lee was the class clown. He spent so much time trying to make others laugh that he never got his work done.*

* *Lisa seemed to disappear into the room. She was a quiet, well-behaved student who never put her hand up when the teacher asked questions. People assumed that she was timid by nature.*

* *Nguyen was just the opposite. He talked all the time. Teachers had a hard time getting him to listen and do his work.*

* *Sarah never seemed to get anything finished. She would start out well but soon lost interest in her work and couldn't be bothered to hand it in on time.*

* *Every piece of work James did had to be perfect. If he couldn't get it right the first time he became angry and upset and called himself 'stupid'.*

* *Terri had spent so many years struggling to make sense of school that she was ready to give up. She was beginning to think that she was too dumb to learn anything anyway.*

* *Raj never seemed to have any homework. He told his parents that he had done all his work while he was at school. He wanted to play video games all evening and never answered his parent's questions about what he was learning.*

* *Philip blamed others for his lack of success. They had either made the work too hard, too easy, or it was just plain dumb. It was never his fault that he barely made the grade.*

All these children in fact were bright but they were struggling to get grades that reflected their abilities. They were underachieving.

We all know children who are underachievers.

- They are the students who are getting by in class but could be learning so much more with a little help.

- They are the students who are bright and who 'could do better' – but no one knows how to help them improve their grades

- They are the students who are working hard to keep up and who don't know why learning isn't fun any more

- They are the students who want to learn but are beginning to feel that they can't learn, that learning is too hard

- They are the students who were doing fine one year but start to struggle the next

- They are the students no one understands. No one understands why these bright kids are giving up on learning, beginning to lose their self confidence and motivation, make excuses for not getting work done and avoid talking about their school day.

# Could do better!

In the real world underachievers are often thought of as being slackers, disappointments, failures, and losers. In school they are accused of being late developers, unfocused, unmotivated, lazy, not trying hard enough, maybe even having behavior problems.

And it is not true!

These students often start out trying harder and working longer than other students. Is it any wonder that, as a result, they become unmotivated, lose confidence in their abilities and even start to behave badly?

# Nine out of ten

It has been estimated, because no one really knows, that 25% of students are under-achieving. This means one in four students will never reach their learning potential, get the grades they deserve, go onto the college of their choice and become lifelong learners able to write their own ticket in life.

I disagree. I think there are 90% not 25%.

I have been working with children with learning issues for over 35 years and I estimate that at nine out of ten students are underachieving in school. Nine out of ten students could do better with the right support.

# Why so many?

All children have difficulty learning at some time in their school career and if they don't get the help they need small difficulties quickly and easily become big problems.

Teachers face two difficulties. It is not easy for them to recognize when children are underachieving and even when they do recognize underachievement they may not be sure what to do about it. Most schools and teachers do their best to help children learn. It isn't easy. Teachers have to pay attention as equally as possible to all students in their class and simply do not have the time to focus on just one child's learning difficulties. The amount of attention a teacher can give each day to an individual learner can be measured in minutes. The teacher may be unaware that a 'grey area' student who is not causing any problems in class could be doing much better. As a result such students gradually fall behind.

# Moms know

The more I work with parents the more I have come to trust a mother's (or father's) instinct about a child's learning.

Moms know when their child is unhappy in school because he or she is struggling to learn. In fact mothers, and sometimes fathers, often know before teachers. Parents know their children better than anyone else and they can see the subtle, or not so subtle, changes in behavior that tell them something is not quite right.

At the same time, children are very good at disguising learning problems. Often the first signs of learning difficulties get overlooked and, when this happens, a learning difficulty may turn into a problem that is hard to fix.

All children underachieve at some time during their school careers and usually short-term underachievement, such as a poor grade on one assignment, has no lasting effects on overall success. But when students underachieve on a regular or semi-regular basis the consequences can be severe.

Remember, if you *think* there is a problem there probably is. Trust your instincts and do what you can to get your child the support he or she needs.

# Lost futures

Underachievement that goes undetected or that does not get addressed inevitably leads to long-term consequences. These consequences include costs to the individual concerned, his or her family, the school and the nation.

The cost to the individual includes a loss of confidence in his or her ability to learn. Children can get into the downward spiral of not getting the grades they expected to get, feeling that no matter how hard they try nothing is going to get better, and losing the motivation they need for the next task. They are on the slope that leads to failure.

There are more pragmatic costs linked to underachievement. If a child's downward spiral continues there is a chance the child will drop out of school or, after graduating, not get higher qualifications. Without these qualifications a person has less chance of getting a full time job and even with a job will be earning much less than the person who is qualified.

According to the US Bureau of Labor Statistics of 2014 there is a 9% unemployment rate for students who do not finish high school. This drops to 3.5% for those who do. Even when employed, students without some kind of post school qualification earn $880 per week compared to the $1101 per week that college graduates earn. That difference in income accounts for about $1.3 million over a working life.

Lack of earning power is not the only consequence of underachievement in school. The loss of self-confidence and self-esteem can lead to behavior that some would call delinquent. Girls without a high school diploma are more likely to become young mothers, as many as 67% of mothers aged 15-17 never finished high school and 68% of prisoners in goal do not have a high school diploma.

The cost to students is enormous but the cost to families can also be high. Parents tell me of sleepless nights worrying about their child's future, hours spent helping with homework, the stress of trying to be a parent and a teacher to their child. They are exhausted by the effort of running a home and supporting their child's education. Their relationship with their child is poor because they feel that they have to be constantly pushing the child to try harder, to complete work on time, to pay attention to the teacher. Supporting your child's education should not come at the cost of family and personal time.

And the tragedy is these costs can be avoided.

Schools also experience the cost of children who are underachieving. Teachers feel stressed because they do not know why some children are finding it difficult to learn. They feel under pressure to get through the curriculum while trying to help students who are slipping behind. The cost of supporting these students in school is prohibitive. Schools may have money to provide extra resources for some children, usually those with obvious and severe learning difficulties, but there never seems to be enough resources to meet the demand. When I was supporting students with learning difficulties I was able to work with 25 out of a school of over 500 and I always had a long waitlist of students needing my support.

Students who underachieve are not going to be able to contribute to the national economy. Some companies are already complaining about a lack of qualified people to take well paying jobs. With a little extra support these students would be ready and able to fill for these jobs and contribute to society.

Children who drop out of school are more likely to get into trouble with the law. This leads to costs associated with more policing and support services for the people who are frustrated with their lives and are causing concerns to society.

If schools and teachers are struggling to provide the support students need is there anywhere else students can get this support?

Yes, there is a resource waiting to be used, a resource that is already doing what it can to help these children but which, without some advice and support, is working largely in the dark. YOU are the resource that can provide the missing piece in children's education, and this book suggests how you can provide this missing piece and how you can remedy the lack of support for your child's learning.

For most sections of this book I provide some practical steps that connect the content to your personal situation. At the end of this section I provide a checklist to discover if YOUR child has a learning difficulty that is stopping him or her reaching their full potential. Knowing your child has difficulty in learning is the first step to getting your child the help he or she needs, help that can make the difference between school success or school failure.

Read the descriptions in Worksheet 1 below, decide which apply to your child, and then calculate your child's score and discover whether your child is reaching his or her learning potential.

# Summary

- The crisis in education is caused by many children not getting the support they need to do well in school

- There are more 'grey area' students than are generally acknowledged

- Parents are often the first to know when a child is struggling to learn

- Many children are not getting the support they need

- There is a difference between short term and long-term underachievement

- There are enormous hidden costs to families, schools and nations as well as to the learner of long-term underachievement

- Schools can't do it all. Children need support from parents as well as teachers – but it must be the right support

# Is your child struggling to learn?

Read each statement and decide whether it describes your child 'always', 'sometimes' or 'never'. The check the appropriate box.

| | Always | Sometimes | Never |
|---|---|---|---|
| **Your child....** | | | |
| Says school is boring | | | |
| Leaves schoolwork till the last minute | | | |
| Produces messy, untidy work | | | |
| Gets grades that are lower than you think he or she should be getting | | | |
| Says they are stupid and cannot learn | | | |
| Leaves homework books at school | | | |
| Has few friends in school | | | |
| Is not happy to go to school | | | |
| Is always tired in the morning | | | |
| Doesn't listen to you | | | |
| Is disorganized | | | |
| Is losing self confidence | | | |
| Insists that work has to be done perfectly | | | |
| Takes the role of the class clown | | | |
| Will not talk about what he or she is learning | | | |
| Gets minor aches and pains on schooldays | | | |
| Avoids doing school-type work | | | |
| Tries hard but never seems to do well | | | |
| Is unwilling to read | | | |
| **TOTAL** | | | |

(continued)

| You ... | Always | Sometimes | Never |
|---|---|---|---|
| Are concerned about your child's education | | | |
| Think your child is lazy | | | |
| Have considered getting help from a tutor | | | |
| Think your child could do better | | | |
| Are concerned about your child's grades | | | |
| Try to help with homework | | | |
| Wonder why your child is not doing as well as you expect | | | |
| Get frustrated when your child will not listen to your advice | | | |
| Know your child is trying hard to do their work | | | |
| Want to spend less time helping with homework | | | |
| Do some of your child's work for him or her | | | |
| Wonder what the teacher is teaching your child | | | |
| Know that your child is bright | | | |
| Wonder why your child is not learning well | | | |
| **TOTAL** | | | |

| Your child's teacher says he or she ... | | | |
|---|---|---|---|
| Is doing as well as can be expected | | | |
| Needs to try harder | | | |
| Needs extra support | | | |
| Lacks focus | | | |
| Will soon catch up | | | |
| Doesn't finish work on time | | | |
| Is slow to start work | | | |
| Could do better | | | |
| Needs to practice | | | |
| Must pay more attention in class | | | |
| **TOTAL** | | | |

Add the totals for 'always' and 'sometimes' to get a final score.

**Final score** _____

## What the score means.

0-10    Congratulations! Your child is doing well and he or she has little difficulty learning. But take care. If grades start to slip or your child stops being an eager happy student you need to discover what has happened and what you can do to help. Working through the Porter Process (described below) will help you understand how to help your child reach even higher for greater school success.

11 – 30.    Your child is struggling to learn. He or she has some learning difficulties that are preventing them from reaching their full learning potential. The Porter Process will help you discover what they are and how to fix them before they become major problems

31-45.    Your child has problems learning and needs your help now. Working through the Porter Process you will discover exactly what support your child needs and how you can prevent your child's downward spiral.

However well your child learns, or whatever difficulties he or she may have the Porter Process will show you how to ensure your child gets the support that leads to learning.

# 2.

# The Porter Process

## What you will learn

- This research based process gives you the power to make a difference in your child's learning life

- It is designed to help parents meet children's unique learning needs

- The five steps that make up the Porter Process

- How these five steps lead to your child's Ultimate Success Formula

## Why this information is important

- The Porter Process is a way parents can ensure they are supporting their child's education in ways that work. It is designed to help parents avoid spending time, money and effort on support that is ineffective and that might even prevent children learning.

So what is the Porter Process and how can it help?

The Porter Process is about parent power. It is a way parents can get the power they need to make a difference in their child's learning lives. It is the result of years working with parents helping them help children learn. It is a powerful tool that all parents can use to ensure they are giving their child the support that leads to learning. It is a way to ensure that 'grey area' students, those students who are underachieving in school, get the support they need and deserve.

The five-step Porter Process is based on sound educational research into how children learn, why some children struggle to reach their full learning potential, and how parents can provide support that helps children overcome learning blocks to be all that they can be. It is not a cookie-cutter solution but a process that helps parent understand their child's unique learning needs and how they can meet those specific needs.

The Porter Process has been used with hundreds of families and helped them discover how to lead their child to learning.

And it can help you too.

# The 5-step Porter Process in a nutshell

Here is an overview of the five steps that will help you create your child's Ultimate Formula for Success – the proven, practical strategies that will help your child overcome learning difficulties and unlock his or her potential.

## 1. Decide on a destination

Get off to a flying start by identifying crystal clear learning goals that are a perfect match for your child, so you can put him or her on a more certain path to success in learning.

## 2. Map the Route

Save time, money and effort, and months of dead ends, by identifying your child's core learning difficulty. Knowing this is the key that unlocks your child's potential.

## 3. Plan the Path

Set the course for success by choosing the perfect strategy to address their core learning difficulty, and by crafting a powerful plan to implement this strategy.

## 4. Take the path

See results quickly by adapting the chosen strategy to your child's learning goals, and by keeping your child on course for success.

## 5. Go further

Review and Renew - what can you do to make success happen more quickly and more easily?

Each of these steps is described in detail in section 2 of this book. As you complete each step you will be adding to a section of your child's unique Ultimate Success Formula, the plan of action that will unlock your child's learning potential. Below I provide a method to enable you to do this.

I suggest that you create a copy of the Ultimate Success Formula (or download it at **http://www.vnaya.com/eonline/users/worksheets**) so you can fill it in as you complete each step.

# Leading to Learning and Vnaya

I take full responsibility for the process described in this book. It is the result of many years looking for a way to help parents make a difference in children's education. As you go through the process and complete the action steps you will come across references to leadingtolearning.com and Vnaya.com. and I need to explain why.

Leading to Learning is the name of my company, a business that is dedicated to providing parents with the advice and information to help children learn. Vnaya is a separate, but related, company that is hosting the links in this book and that provides a range of services to parents.

The CEO of this company approached me because he wanted to extend the services he offered to parents and was interested in my work. To make a long story short we found we had the same beliefs and ideas about the importance of parents in helping children and we are now working together to provide parents with advice and information so all children can reach their learning potential.

I still work individually with parents but I have also trained a group of dedicated professionals to provide the support you need. You can access these at **www.Vnaya.com.** These Learning Leaders can guide you through the Porter Process and help you unlock your child's learning potential.

I am fortunate that Vnaya has agreed to host links from this book. These links allow you to download the action worksheets and give you access to detailed information about children's learning.

Vnaya also provides on-line tutoring. The tutors at Vnaya are special in that they know about learning styles and learning skills and can use them to make tutoring more beneficial for your child. Vnaya also hosts a free diagnostic learning assessment that I developed that you can access immediately to discover your child's learning skills and learning preferences. I refer to this in step 3 of the process and it is an integral part of helping you discover your child's learning needs.

When you take this assessment – it only takes a few minutes and your get results immediately – you will automatically receive my weekly newsletter in which I give practical tips on ways to enhance learning and advance notice of courses and special offers.

This book stands on its own, but the relationship between Vnaya and Leading to Learning changes it into a powerful tool that can benefit all parents and children.

## Summary

- The Porter Process gives parents the power to make a difference in their child's lives. The five steps lead to a Success Formula that is tailored to the specific needs of the child and family.

# Your Child's Ultimate Success Formula

**Step 1.** Set the destination – decide on a learning goal
My learning goal for my child is __

**Step 2.** Map the route – Discover learning needs
My child needs support to …

| Learn how to learn | Makes school make sense | Move to mastery |
|:---:|:---:|:---:|
| ☐ | ☐ | ☐ |

Results of Assessment at www.Vnaya.com

| Skills my child needs | My child's learning preferences | Type of support |
|---|---|---|
| _____ | _____ | _____ |
| _____ | _____ | _____ |
| _____ | _____ | _____ |

**Step 3.** Plan the Path  - Chosen Strategies

Standard Strategy - _____

_____

Super Strategy  - _____

_____

Specific Strategies – _____

_____

**Step 4.** Take the road to success.  Create Success strategies

Standard to Success – _____

_____

Super to Success – _____

_____

Specific to Success – _____

_____

## **Step 5.** – Go further

Review – _____

_____

Renew – _____

_____

# 3.

# Gambling with kids' futures

## What you will learn

- Why supporting your child's education can be stressful, and frustrating

- Why most parents guess what support their child needs

- The problems with guessing

- Whether you are helping your child in ways that work

## Why this information is important

- Many parents find supporting their child's education is hard work. They become stressed, exhausted, and even angry and the parent/child relationship starts to suffer. This chapter shows you why this happens and what you can do to stop it happening.

Most parents know they have a role to play in helping children succeed in school and they try to provide the support their child's needs. I have met many parents who were doing their best to help their child get better grades, pass exams, catch up missing lessons and get a head start on the school year.

I have also known many parents who were frustrated, exhausted, stressed, confused and even angry because despite all the time, money and energy they were putting into providing support, nothing seemed to be working.

During my research I interviewed many parents all of whom were doing their best to support their children. They each had their own ideas about what type of support would help their child but they knew that the support they were offering was either not working well or not working at all. Parents were doing their best to support their child's education but it wasn't working and they didn't know why.

After talking to parents it didn't take me long to work out why they were having such a hard time. They were guessing what support their child needed and their guesses were based on wrong or incomplete information. It was easy to understand why these parents had to guess. Home/school communication was poor so parents were not getting much advice from teachers, the media was full of cookie-cutter silver bullets that promised wonderful results, and their friends were sharing information about the amazing tutors and resources they were using with their children. What else could parents do but guess what type of support would work for their child?

But guessing is not the best approach to take.

# The problem with guessing

When parents guess what support their child needs three things tend to happen.

1. **Children get 'too much school'**
   Parents value school learning over home learning. They value a teacher's contribution to their child's education more than their own. This leads to parents spending hours helping with homework, hiring tutors, buying workbooks – all 'school type' learning activities.

   There is nothing wrong with any of these actions if they meet a child's learning needs but parents rush to provide 'more school' before they have explored other ways of meeting their child's learning needs.  Also giving a child 'more school' can mean that the child is missing the special learning opportunities that only parents can provide. Children may be getting 'too much school' and not enough 'parent'.

2. **Symptoms may be cured but the cause remains**
   When you are in pain you want your doctor to find out why you are in pain so he can prescribe the medicine that will make you better. You want the pain to go away but you really need the doctor to get to the root of the problem so the pain does not come back. Curing symptoms only is a short-term solution to a long-term problem. Guessing what support your child needs might cure your child's learning symptoms but it will not get at the root of the problem and create a long-term cure.

3. **You may be putting the cart before the horse**
   This is a British expression that means doing things in the wrong order.  Putting the cart before the horse means working in ways that are counterproductive and inefficient and that just don't work! When you guess what support your child needs you may be doing just that. You may be expecting your child to learn math when he doesn't understand some basic math principles.  You may be trying to teach your child to write a book report when she doesn't have the skills to understand what the book was about. When you guess what support your child needs you may put the cart before the horse, you may be expecting your child to learn before he or she knows how to learn.

4. **You ignore your special skills**
   You have a much greater chance of success when you do something you are good at doing rather than trying to do something you are not sure about. Giving your child

'more school' is not playing to your strength as a parent. Fulfilling the special role you have as a parent leads to less stress and more satisfaction as well as better learning for your child. The following are examples of parents' efforts, with the successful outcome resulting from the Porter Process.

*Paula was spending three hours every night helping her daughter with homework. She was desperate and her family life was a wreck. She knew that she couldn't go on this way but she had no idea what else she could do.*

*When she discovered her daughter needed to learn how to plan her work she was able to help her learn how to do this. Now homework help takes less than 30 minutes.*

*Mr. D sent his son to a tutoring program that guaranteed success. However his son hated it and didn't do the homework. Despite the guarantee Mr. D knew he had wasted his money.*

*He learned what type of program would work for his son. Now he knows his money is well spent.*

*Mrs. P wanted to help her young daughter learn to read. She had seen a TV advertisement about a learning to read program and decided to buy it. It was expensive but she knew it was important for her daughter to read and she didn't know how to help her do this. When the materials arrived it was not what she was expecting. The instructions were complicated and she didn't have the time needed to use them well. She soon abandoned the program.*

*Now she knows what skills her daughter needs and is using read-together time to help develop them.*

*Ms. R knew that her daughter was bright but she was struggling in school and needed help. She tried helping her daughter by getting copies of her schoolbooks so she could review the work at home. But it didn't work. Her daughter resented having to do more schoolwork in the evenings and relationships were getting stressed. Her daughter was getting more and more behind in class.*

*Ms. R discovered she was trying to help her Picture Smart daughter in Word Smart ways. A change of strategy lead to improved relationships, less stress and more homework getting finished.*

*Mr. and Mrs. W were worried about their teenage son. He was a bright boy but he was not happy at school and he never seemed to do any work at home despite both of them trying to motivate him to get his work finished. The situation at home was tense. Parents were worried and stressed and the boy was uncommunicative and stubborn.*

*They discovered their Music and Picture Smart son preferred a less traditionally structured school environment and after a year in a Community College he won a full scholarship to the university of his choice.*

## Summary

- There is no need to become stressed and exhausted when you support your child's education. When you understand what your child needs to learn you can tailor support and make it happen.

Are you guessing what support your child needs? Take this parental support assessment to discover if what you are doing is helping your child.

## Parental Support Assessment

Answer yes or no to each question.

| | Y | N |
|---|---|---|
| Are you completely happy with the support you offer? | | |
| Are you sure you are providing exactly what your child needs? | | |
| Does your child appreciate your support? | | |
| Does s/he agree that this is the help s/he needs right now? | | |
| Are you happy with the amount of time you spend helping your child? | | |
| Are you happy with the amount of money you are spending to provide support? | | |
| Do you think you are getting value for the money you spend? | | |
| Does the effort you spend helping your child seem worth it? | | |
| Do you get the results you want? | | |
| Do you help your child because you want to, not because you feel pressured? | | |
| Do you avoid becoming frustrated when you help your child? | | |
| Does your child avoid becoming frustrated when you are working with him/her? | | |
| Do you avoid the pressure to do some of your child's homework? | | |
| Do you know exactly how to help your child? | | |
| Does your child appreciate your help? | | |

| | Y | N |
|---|---|---|
| Do you notice your child learning? | | |
| Do you feel confident that your support is making a difference? | | |
| Do you have enough time with family? | | |
| Have you asked your child's teacher what help s/he needs? | | |
| Do you know how your child likes to learn? | | |
| Do you know what your child needs to learn? | | |
| Have you found the right way to help your child? | | |
| Is providing support stress free? | | |
| Is your child happy to ask you for your support? | | |
| Do you have enough time for yourself? | | |

Score one point each time you answered 'yes'                    Score _____

## What your score means

**20 or more:** Well done! You are giving your child what he or she needs to succeed. I congratulate you because I know how hard you are working at giving your child a great future. However there may be easier and less stressful ways to help your child succeed. The Porter Process can help you find them.

**15-20:** You are doing some things right! You might consider concentrating on the ways that work best and dropping those that are more trouble than they are worth. The Porter Process can help you find them.

**Below 15:** A low score does not mean you are a bad parent or you do not care about your child's education. It usually means that you are trying too hard! You, like many parents, are spending time and effort helping your child but not getting results. The Porter Process is for you. Go through the five steps to make helping your child stress free and effective.

# 4.

# Parents are important

## What you will learn

- Parents have a vital role to play in helping your child succeed in school

- They need to set the scene for learning

- Three ways they can do this

## Why this information is important

- When you understand your role in leading your child to learning you can provide support to meet your child's specific learning needs and ensure that he or she reaches their full potential

Getting a good education is important and schools can't do it all.

But there is good news. As important as teachers are to a child's education they are not the most important factor in a child's success. The person who has the most influence on a child's success in school is you – the parent.  Research has shown that much of a child's success depends on how parents interact with their children at home.

Your child needs your support.

 To be successful, children need support from both a caring teacher and a loving parent. Parents and teachers have different roles to play in helping children learn.  We know what teachers must do –teach what is in the curriculum – and hopefully do it in ways that help children learn. But what is the role of the parent?  Parents are not usually trained teachers and even if they are they should not confuse their parenting role with their teaching role.

After talking to hundreds of parents and teachers about the difference between these two roles I came to a conclusion that seems obvious and that alters how we view education's missing piece.

A parent's role is **to set the scene for learning so that children can benefit from the work teachers do in school, as well as ensuring their child learns from the many opportunities offered in daily life**.

Let me explain what 'setting the scene' means. When you watch a play or a TV drama the background, the scenery, provides you with information about where and when the action is taking place. You are given a context that helps you understand what is happening. Someone has put a lot of time and thought into the setting by choosing what shots to take or creating the scenery and digital effects that make this happen. Without this carefully chosen scenery there could be a disconnect between the actions and where the action is taking place. Imagine watching a sword fight in a bathroom or a car chase in a serene flower garden! It wouldn't seem right and the viewer would be left wondering why things were so mixed up and would spend time and energy trying to work things out.

The same happens with learning. Children need the kind of background that helps them make sense of what they are being taught. Children who do not have this background are either trying to learn in a vacuum or in a situation that is confusing to them.

I am sure you have noticed the look on a child's face when he or she is trying to make sense of something you have said. The quizzical look that says 'I am trying to work this out' or the vague look in a child's eyes when he has no idea what you are talking about. Learning needs context. When parents give children the context that allows learning to make sense, children can spend their energies on absorbing information and knowledge.

Fortunately 'setting the scene' for learning is something parents do naturally. Parents are a child's first teacher and before a child goes to school parents have automatically helped their child learn vast amounts of information and knowledge. Parents helped children learn how to walk, talk, socialize and maybe even read. This process is so much a part of childrearing that parents set the scene for learning without even realizing what they are doing. However this lack of realization can create problems. Parents may help children learn some things and not others. As a result some children do not get all the 'scene setting' they need and this can lead to difficulties when the child goes to school. Teachers assume that children know how to learn and are ready to learn. They don't spend much time helping children learn how to learn, unless your child is lucky enough to go to a good kindergarten where he or she will get support to develop the skills that lead to learning.

Experienced and well-trained Kindergarten teachers arrange their classroom schedule in a way that helps children develop the skills they need. For example, there is sharing time, quiet time, listening time, and many other activities that help children learn how to learn. However, even these hard working teachers admit that it is difficult for them to ensure that all the children in their class develop all the skills they need.

I once asked a friend of mine who taught a class of children in kindergarten what she thought about parental support for children's learning. She said that it was vital parents get involved in helping children learn. There was no ambiguity about her belief that parental support is essential to a child's success in school! She told me that she needed parents to help their children learn how to share, how to listen, how to interact with others, how to hold a pencil and many other things so that they would be ready to participate fully in the classroom. She wanted parents to set the scene for learning!

I asked teachers who taught older children how they wanted parents to support their child's education. Did they want parents to help with homework, review what had been taught, give their children more work so they could practice their skills? They didn't really want parents to do any of these things. They said they wanted parents to make sure their child got to school on time well fed and rested, to let them know if their child was having a problem with homework, and to give their child life experiences that would help them better understand what they were teaching. They did not want parents to 'teach' their child new ways of doing their work. They wanted parents to ensure their child was ready and prepared to benefit from their teaching. They were happy to take the responsibility of helping children learn what they taught as long as parents were ensuring their child was ready to learn.

Setting the scene for learning is really important and it is something only parents can do.

## Summary

- Your role is to set the scene for learning so that your child is ready to benefit from the work teachers do.

- Guessing how to support your child leads to stress and frustration

## Are you setting the scene for learning?

List all the ways you are helping your child learn. These could include things like helping with homework, getting books ready for the morning, driving to school, hiring a tutor, being supportive, going to meetings at school, finding space for your child to do homework, buying books, showing him what to do…

Make sure you write down all the ways you are supporting your child's education.

Then go through the list and cross off all the activities that teachers do. This would include showing your child what to do, reminding your child to get work finished, checking your child has done work correctly. If you think an activity is something that a teacher could or should do cross it off.

You will be left with a list of activities that set the scene for learning.

# 5.

# A better way

## What you will learn

- How to take the stress and confusion out of helping your child reach his or her learning potential

- The 5 step process that helps you tailor the support you offer to meet your child's specific learning needs

- How to do this in less time and with less effort than you are using already

## Why it is important

- Your child needs support that meets his or her learning goals. To provide this support you must first discover what your child needs to learn and how to provide support that meets these needs.

Helping your child succeed in school can be enjoyable and rewarding. It can be a time when your child accepts and appreciates your support and feels empowered to move onto further learning. It can be a time when you help your child grow and take his or her place in the world.

It should not be a time you dread, or a time that causes stress and exhaustion, or that leads to upset and anger. But it often is. I tell parents that no amount of help with homework or work with tutors is worth jeopardizing the relationship you have with your child and family.

The one way to prevent this situation and to ensure your child gets the support that leads to success is to discover what your child needs to learn and help him learn it.

In an earlier chapter you learned the signs that tell you whether what you are doing is working or not. Now is the time to discover how to ensure you offer support that makes a positive and long lasting difference in your child's learning life.

And all it takes is five simple steps that will help you discover the secret key that opens the door to your child's future, the future they dream about and the one you want to give them. These are the five steps that the next section will lead you through.

But before we start on the Porter Process itself, there are some things you need to do to get ready and be able to implement it properly. I call this making space for effective learning.

## Summary

The Porter Process gives parents the power to ensure children get the education they need and deserve.

# 6.

# Making Space

## What you will learn

- How much time, energy and effort you are spending on trying to support your child's education

- Which of those activities are working and which are not

- How to stop doing what isn't working and …

- … make room for what will

## Why this information is important

- This book is about providing support for your child that is stress-free and effective. It is not about asking you to do more. It is about expecting you to do less but to make that 'less' really effective. Only when you stop doing what isn't working will you have the space to do what does.

## What you will do

- List all the ways you support your child's education

- Decide which work for you and your child

- Concentrate on those actions that are working

- Stop doing those which are not

At the moment you may be helping with homework, paying for tutoring, buying books and games, creating a workspace, and worrying about what to do next. All these types of support can be useful and can lead to more success in school. So why are you getting frustrated, tired, upset and confused? Why do you think that there must be an easier way to support your child's education?

Because some of the things you are doing are not working, or are not working as well as they could be:

- you think "Oh, not again!" when your child needs help with homework.

- you get annoyed when projects are left till the last minute and you have to find time to help

- your child tells you "that is not the way we were taught to do it"

- you have to remind (nag!) your child once again to start his homework

- you are tired of hearing all the excuses why work does not get done

- you wonder why your child has to do this stupid stuff anyway?

- you don't have enough time to be with the rest of your family

- you are not sure the help you are providing is what your child needs

- your child does not appreciate your support

- you resent the time and money spent getting your child to tutors

- you are doing the same thing every night

- both you and your child end up frustrated and confused

- you end up doing some of your child's homework – because it is quicker

- you think that you are doing the job the teacher should be doing.

These are all signs that what you are doing isn't working. Sometimes some of the ways you try to help your child may actually be stopping him or her learning. And when you are spending time doing what isn't working you are not making time for what will work.

Here is a four-stage process to help you stop doing what isn't working so you can make room for what will.

1.  Make a list of all the ways you are helping your child at the moment. You may have already done this in the first section of this book. You might want to use that list or create a new one now you have a better understanding of your role.

    Include all the things you do around homework help, all the times you talk about schoolwork, the money you spend on resources and tutoring, the amount of time you spend getting your child ready for school, making sure the right book are brought home, checking backpacks. Also include the amount of time you talk to your child about schooling and learning, report card feedback, teacher meetings, PAC meetings

2.  Now look at each item on the list and decide whether it is working for you AND for your child.

     Look at the list above to remind yourself of what 'not working' feels like. Remember to trust your instincts. Cross off all the activities that are not working for you and then cross of the activities that are not working for your child. Ask your child if you are not sure what is working for him or her. You may be left with a very short list of activities that do work – that is fine.

3.  From this short list choose two or three activities that work best, in that they work every time and leave both you and your child feeling good.

4.  STOP doing every other activity but the two or three you have chosen. Concentrate on doing the activities that work. This can be a difficult step for some parents but it is essential if you are going to make time to do what works. Until you have worked through this book and created a truly effective action plan for supporting your child's education I want you to only do those two or three things that work. In fact if you only did one of the activities on the list your child would not suffer and you would find you have the time and energy you need to do other things.

This process will help you realize just how much time, effort and money you are spending on supporting your child's education. Even if your list is short this process will help you understand how you are helping your child and what effect it is having.

Once you have made space for new ways to support your child's education, ways that are designed to meet your child's learning needs, you are ready to start the 5 step Porter Process.

# Linda's story

*When I picked up the phone all I could hear was someone sobbing. A mother told me that she just couldn't do it any more. She couldn't spend hours each night helping her daughter do her homework. She was exhausted and her family life was a mess. She needed help.*

*We set a time to go through the Porter Process and then I helped her decide what she could stop doing until we knew the type of support her daughter needed. This was a big relief for Linda because she saw light at the end of the tunnel; she knew that she could get her life back.*

*Now Linda knows how to help her daughter, homework is completed in less time and everyone is happy. The first step was to make space for what was needed.*

# Summary
-  Stop doing what isn't working so you have space for what will.

## 1. Ways I help my child learn

_____

_____

_____

_____

_____

_____

## 2. Ways I will continue to use

_____

_____

_____

_____

_____

# Section 2

# The Porter Process

| Step 1 | Decide on a learning goal | | |
|---|---|---|---|
| Step 2 | Discover learning needs | | |
| | 1. Learn how to learn | 2. Make school Make Sense | 3. Move to mastery |
| Step 3 | Choose strategies that work | | |
| | 1. Standard Strategy | 2. Super Strategy | 3. Specific Strategy |
| Step 4 | Create Strategies for Success | | |
| | 1. Standard to Success | 2. Super to Success | 3. Specific to Success |
| Step 5 | Celebrate Success | | |
| | Review and renew | | |

# Step 1

# Clarify your concerns and decide on a destination

"Would you tell me, please, which way I ought to go from here?"

"That depends a good deal on where you want to get to," said the Cat.

"I don't much care where—" said Alice.

"Then it doesn't matter which way you go," said the Cat.

"—so long as I get SOMEWHERE," Alice added as an explanation.

"Oh, you're sure to do that," said the Cat, "if you only walk long enough."

from Alice in Wonderland by Lewis Carroll

| Step 1    Decide on a learning goal |
| --- |

## What you will learn

- How to set crystal clear learning goals for your child

## Why this information is important

- With a crystal clear learning goal you know where you want to go

## What you will do

- Think about and describe the change you want to see in your child

- Create a crystal clear learning goal that your child will achieve

- Add this goal to your child's Ultimate Success Formula

A clear learning goal helps you pinpoint the strategies that will help your child and avoid wasting time and money on strategies that don't work, or don't work well. Having a crystal clear goal helps you make sure that the support you offer is simple, easy and effective. You save time, effort and possibly money by eliminating what doesn't work and concentrating on what does.

Many parents have a general learning goal for their child. They want their child to get better grades, to finish homework on time, to work harder. These are all good goals but they are too general to use as the basis of an efficient, effective learning program.

For instance here are some general goals and why they are incomplete

- 'To get better grades'  - what grade do you want your child to reach? Do you want him or her to get better grades in all subjects or just one? When do you want him or her to get better grades – at the end of the school year or next week?

- To get homework done on time - What homework? How long should your child take to do this?  Everyday? What does finished homework look like?

- To do more work – How much more work?  What kind of work?  How are you going to measure the amount of work? What is the goal that this extra work will achieve?

When you are clear about your destination you can plan the best way to get there! So the question to ask is – How can I make general learning goals more specific so that I have a particular destination in mind and can focus all my efforts – and my child's efforts – on getting there?

It is not as difficult as you might think.

Here are a two ways to create crystal clear learning goals for your child so that you can ensure the support you offer is not going to be wasted.

## 1 'Paint a Picture'

This approach to goal setting works well for parents who are mainly Picture Smart. These parents find it easy to create pictures in their heads but it can work for others too.

Try to remember the last time you were concerned about your child's learning.  It may have been last night or it may have been last week. Then 'paint a picture' in your mind's eye of exactly what was happening at that time. Where were you? What time was it? What were you doing? What was your child doing? Try to make the picture as complete and as clear as possible. Take a few minutes to do this – don't rush – you need to get this picture clear before you move onto the next part of this exercise.

When you are sure that you have 'painted a picture' about the situation put it aside for a moment.

Now I want you to paint another picture in your mind.  This time I want you to think of the same situation but paint a picture of what it would look like if everything went well, if your child was doing what you wanted him or her to do.

What changed? What did your child do in the second picture that he or she didn't do in the first? Try to describe the change as carefully as possible.

That change is your learning goal. The difference between what your child did in the first 'picture' and what he or she did in the second 'picture' is what you want your child to achieve. It is your learning goal for your child.

The more detailed the picture you create the clearer the learning goal will be.

Here are some examples -

*Debbie wasn't sure what her learning goal was for her son. She told me that she knew he was not keeping up in class and felt this was because he was not motivated to do his work.*

*When she 'painted a picture' by thinking about the last time she had been upset by her son's behavior she was able to pinpoint a situation that was causing her, and her son, to get upset. It had been that morning as she waited to drive him to school. He wasn't ready and he was making excuses for not being ready on time.  They had argued.*

*When she 'painted a picture' of what she would like to happen she pictured her son being ready on time and eager to get to school. She felt that this would ensure that the whole family had a better start to the day. This mother had other learning goals but that was the one she wanted to achieve first.*

*What had changed? In the second picture she knew exactly what she wanted from her child. After going through the Porter Process, she was able to plan how to motivate him to be ready for school every day of the week.*

*When she learned the strategies she could use to achieve this she was amazed at the result. Within two days her son was not only ready on time every day but he was often waiting for her! Now this mother is working on her second learning goal.*

Here is another example.

*Mr. and Mrs. S were worried that their son would not get into college. They knew he was bright but he was just not getting the grades that would get him into the college of his choice. Also they knew that he was unhappy in school but didn't know what to do about it.*

*The first picture they painted showed a situation that was very stressful for all concerned. It showed them trying to motivate their son to do his work, trying to make sure that he finished it and handed it in on time.*

*The second picture showed their son happy, playing the music he loved, getting his work done with no fuss and getting the grades they knew he was capable of getting.*

*What had changed?*

*Their son had become a happy eager learner who was enjoying his life while working hard in a school he loved.*

*The parents now had a crystal clear learning goal – to find a school that their son would be happy to attend and that could meet their child's learning needs. When they discovered, through the Porter Process, that their child was mainly Picture Smart and Music Smart they were able to move him into a less traditional school where his learning needs were met more appropriately.*

*At the end of the school year parents told me that their son had won a full scholarship to the college of his choice.*

The second way to create crystal clear goals uses a more analytical approach. This approach is useful for parents who are Word Smart or Number Smart.

In fact this approach uses the letters S.M.A.R.T. as a guideline.

## 2. SMART Goals

These are the initials for the steps you can take to help you create a crystal clear learning goal.

## S is for Specific

Your goal needs to be as specific as possible -

## M is for Measurable

How will you measure success?

## A is for Achievable

Is this something that you could reasonably expect your child to achieve?

## R is for Realistic

The goal must be something you both want to achieve. It cannot be something imposed on your child.

## T is for Timely

How long is it going to take to achieve?

For example –

> *Karim's parents wanted him to get better grades in school. They knew he was struggling to learn even though he was bright and capable of getting good grades. This was a good general goal but it needed to be made crystal clear. By going through the SMART process their learning goal became to help John increase his grade in Math (specific) from a C to a B (measurable) before the end of the school year (timely). They knew that Karim wanted to do better in Math (realistic) and that an improvement of one grade was possible (realistic).*

> *Once this more detailed goal was identified, and after using the free diagnostic learning assessment developed by and for the Porter Process the parents hired a tutor who understood what learning skills Karim needed to develop (planning and production) and how he learned best (visually). Karim's end of year report not only included a B in math but in a couple of other subjects as well!*

Another example –

> *Rupinder's teacher said that her grades would improve if she focused more on her work. After talking to her teacher the parents were able to change this general goal into a SMART goal. They wanted Rupinder to pay attention (specific) to what she had to do by concentrating on understanding instructions (measurable). They knew Rupinder could do this if she was reminded about doing it (achievable) and that she wanted to get better marks (realistic). They wanted this to happen within a few days (timely). With this crystal clear goal they were able to learn specific strategies through the Porter Process to make this happen.*

Once you are happy that you have a **crystal clear learning goal** for your child – and this may be only the first goal of many – you are ready to move onto the next step of the process – finding the type of support your child needs.

## Summary

- Learning goals need to be crystal clear
- Learning goals are the change you want to see in your child
- Using S.M.A.R.T. as a guideline will help you create a clear learning goal

# Worksheet #1
## Paint a picture

1. Describe the last time you were concerned about your child's learning. Where were you? What time was it? What was your child doing? What were you doing? Had either of you done this before? How did you feel? How did your child feel?

2. Paint a picture of what you would have liked to happen. What would you do? What would your child do? Why would this matter?

3. What changed? What did your child do that was different from the first picture? What did you do that was different?

4. Write down this change as a general learning goal. This will be the first of many learning goals so do not worry about it being 'too small'.

# Worksheet #2

## Crystal clear learning goal

Can you make your learning goals more clear?

*Specific* – can you envision exactly what you want to happen?

*Measurable* – how will you measure success?

*Attainable* – will your child be able to do this?

*Realistic* – do you both want it to happen?

*Timely* – how long before you wan this to be achieved?

My crystal clear learning goal

# Step 2

# Find the best route

'It's impossible to map out a route to your destination
if you don't know where you're starting from'.

Suze Orman

| Step 2     Discover learning needs | | |
|---|---|---|
| 1. Learn how to learn | 2. Make school Make Sense | 3. Move to mastery |

## What you will learn

- How to discover what type of support your child needs.

## Why this information is important

- To be effective the support you offer your child has to match where your child is in the learning process. Otherwise you could be wasting your time, money and energy and may even be preventing your child learning.

## What you will do

- Complete a questionnaire to discover where your child needs support

- Discover which skills your child might need to learn, and how your child prefers to learn, by taking a free learning assessment specially designed for the Porter Process at http://www.Vnaya.com

- Add this information to your child's Ultimate Success Formula

Now that you have a clear goal the next step is to decide what type of support will help you reach that goal. Knowing what type of support your child needs means that you can lead him or her along the path to their learning goal. This will help you avoid paths that will not get you to where you want to go.

Children may need support in one or more of three stages of learning – **learning how to learn, making sense of school and moving to mastery©**.

Many children struggle to learn because they have not developed the skills that enable them to learn. They have not learned *how* to learn. Learning *how* to learn is the first, and most important, stage of a child's learning life. They need support that helps them develop the skills they need.

Other children do not reach their full learning potential because the way they are taught does not match the way they learn. These children struggle to make sense of school. *Making sense of school* is the second stage in the process of learning. These children need support that helps them adapt how they are being taught to how they like to learn.

The third stage of learning is when children master what they are taught and can demonstrate their learning by getting good grades, passing examinations, and moving on. In order to *move to mastery* children may need extra support from parents and tutors.

Complete the questionnaire at the end of this section to discover your child's learning needs.

Add this information to Step 2 of your child's Ultimate Success Formula. You have now completed the first part of Step 2.

Knowing the type of support your child needs is important but it is does not give you the detailed information you need to choose the strategies that will lead to success. You need to discover what skills your child needs to develop, how your child prefers to learn and what type of support your child needs to Move to Mastery.

Use the free on-line Diagnostic Learning Assessment at www.Vnaya.com (if you haven't already done so) to discover which skills your child needs to develop and how your child prefers to learn.

Add this information to the second part of Step 2 of your child's Ultimate Success Formula.

The free assessment gives you information about your child's learning preferences and learning skills but it does not tell you what type of support your child needs to Move to Mastery. If your child needs support in this stage of learning it may be one or more of the following three types.

1. Catch up

     Your child might need support to catch up on work because of missed lessons, illness or change of school. Children might need help to catch up on learning if they have been struggling to learn and have fallen behind in class. This type of support can be provided at the same time as support in the other stages of learning but it does need careful choice of a tutor or tutoring program and good communication between you and the tutor so you can explain what your child's learning needs are at other stages of learning.

2.  Accelerated learning

    Your child might need support to accelerate learning so he or she can get good marks on exams or to prepare your child for the next grade.

3.  New learning

    Your child might need support learning a new subject, a subject that is not provided by the school. Many parents for whom English is a second language want their children to be proficient in their first language and use tutors to help children learn this language. You may want your child to learn to play musical instrument or go to ballet class.

Choose which type of support your child needs and add this information to the second part of Step 2 of your child's Ultimate Success Formula

# Summary

- To be effective the support you offer your child has to match his or her learning needs. A child may have needs at one or more of the three stages of learning described above. By discovering which stage a child needs support parents can choose strategies that meet that learning need.

# Discover your child's learning needs

Answer each set of questions. Score one point each time you answer yes. Find your total for each set. The results indicate the type of support your child needs.

## Set A

- Has your child been struggling to learn for some time?

- Does your child need help in more than one subject?

- Have you tried to help but nothing you do seems to work?

- Does your child try hard to learn but makes little progress?

- Is your child getting anxious and upset about their ability to learn?

Score Set A _____

**If you score 4 or more your child needs support at the first stage of learning – to learn how to learn.**

To discover which learning skills your child needs to develop take the free Diagnostic Learning assessment at www.Vnaya.com. You will get results within minutes and will learn which skills your child needs.

## Set B

- Has your child changed schools or teacher recently?

- Does your child learn more from some teachers than others?

- Has your child moved between grades 3 and 4 or Grades 7 and 8?

- Do you know your child 'could do better'?

- Have your child's grades only started dropping in the last year?

## Score Set B _____

**If you score 4 or more your child needs support at the middle stage of learning – making school make sense.**

To discover how your child learns and how his or her learning style relates to learning in school take the free Diagnostic Learning assessment at www.Vnaya.com. You will get results within minutes and discover your child's learning style and strategies to adapt the way your child is being taught to the way he or she learns best.

## Set C

- Is your child doing OK in school but you think that he could do better with extra support?

- Is your child bored by the work he is given to do?

- Does your child need help in a specific subject?

- Has your child been absent from school and missed some lessons?

- Do you want to help your child prepare for an exam or test?

## Score Set C _____

**If you score 4 or more your child needs support at the last stage of learning – move to mastery**

To get immediate access to tutors that teach the way your child learns go to www. Vnaya.com and check out the on line tutoring services.

# Step 3 -

# Plan the Path

'A goal without a plan is just a wish.'
Antoine de Saint Exupery

| Step 3    Choose strategies that work | | |
|---|---|---|
| 1. Standard  Strategy | 2. Super Strategy | 3. Specific Strategy |

## What you will learn

- The types of strategies you can use to help your child learn

- How to choose and use strategies

## Why this information is important

- Knowing what your child needs to learn is useless unless you know what you can do to help.

## What you will do

- Choose one strategy from each of the three sets of strategies in the resource section of this book to use with your child.

In this step you set the course for success by choosing the perfect strategies that addresses your child's core learning issues. These strategies are listed in the third section of the book. There are three sets of strategies to choose from.

**1.** Standard Strategies

These are strategies parents may use throughout a child's life to support learning, strategies such as rewarding a child in ways that motivate and develop self-confidence.

**2.** Super Strategies

These strategies relate to specific learning needs. They are strategies you can use to help your child in each of the three stages of learning - **Learn how to Learn, Make Sense of School,** or **Move to Mastery**. Your child may have learning needs in more than one of these areas.

**3.** Specific Strategies

There are hundreds of specific strategies in this section of the book. These are strategies that relate to the development of specific learning skills, learning preferences and the provision of extra support. You may want to glance at them all but you need to look carefully at the ones that relate to your child's specific learning needs.

# How to choose strategies

**1.** First choose a Standard Strategy

Look at the list of Standard Strategies and choose one that you will start to use immediately. If you are already using one or more of these strategies with your child there is no need to change what you are doing unless you want to.

For instance you may already be rewarding your child for doing something well (Brownie Points) but might also help your child's self confidence by seeing failure as a learning opportunity.

Add any new strategy to your child's Ultimate Success Formula.

**2.** Then choose a Super Strategy

Look at the Super Strategies that relate to the stages of learning in which your child needs support.

If your child needs support in more than one stage of learning look at the strategies in the earlier stage of learning first. For instance, if your child needs support to Make school make sense and to Move to mastery choose strategies that help Make school make sense. You can always use the Move to Mastery strategies at a later date.

Add your chosen Super Strategy to your child's Ultimate Success Formula.

You have now chosen two strategies that will help you set the scene for the support you are going to offer. The next set of learning strategies – Specific Strategies – will help you meet your child's specific learning needs.

Before you can choose Specific Strategies to help your child you need the results of the Porter Diagnostic Learning Assessment. These results will tell you what skills your child needs to develop and how your child prefers to learn. This assessment is free, takes only a few minutes to complete and can be found at www.Vnaya.com

**3.** Choose Specific Strategies

Now we come to the strategies you can use to develop a specific area of your child's learning.

If your child needs to Learn how to Learn look for the skill your child needs to develop and choose a strategy from that section. For instance if your child needs to learn how to pay attention look at section learn how to learn and read the strategies you can use to develop that skill.

If your child needs to Make School Make Sense find your child's main learning preference and choose a strategy you will use. For instance if your child is a Picture Smart learner look in the section Make School Make Sense for the strategies you can use with Picture Smart learners.

If your child needs to Move to Mastery choose one or more of the strategies in the section that relates to your child's needs. For instance if your child needs help to catch up his or her learning find that section and read the strategies you can use to make this happen.

<u>Add to the chosen strategies to Step 3 of your child's Ultimate Success Formula.</u>

Now you have chosen three strategies that can use to help your child become a better learner and succeed in school. You do not have to ignore the other strategies in the resource section of the book you can use them later. It is better to start with a few strategies so you have time and space to use them well rather than several strategies that you do not feel confident using.

In the next step you are going to link your chosen strategies to the learning goal you have set.

# Step 4 -

# Take the path to Success

'Success is nothing more than a few simple disciplines
practiced every day.'

Jim Rohn

| Step 4 | Create Strategies for Success | |
|---|---|---|
| 1. Standard to Success | 2. Super to Success | 3. Specific to Success |

## What you will learn

- How to see results fast by adapting the chosen strategy to meet your learning goals, and keep your child on course to their amazing future.

## Why this is important

- Only you know what you want your child to achieve. By adapting the strategies to help you reach that goal you are ensuring your child's success.

## What you will do

- Take the strategies you chose in Step 3 and create Success Strategies by adjusting them help you reach your learning goal.

- Start using these Success Strategies with your child

Now you have a crystal clear learning goal for your child, you have identified his or her core learning issue and chosen a strategy that addresses that issue. You have one more step to take. You need to adapt the strategies you have chosen to the learning goal you have set.

Then you will have strategies that not only meet your child's learning needs but also ensure he or she reaches the learning goals you have set.

This is not as difficult as it may seem as all the Strategies are designed to be useful in many situations.

1.  How to adjust Standard Strategies to Success Strategies

Take the Standard Strategy you chose and link it to your learning goal. Here are some examples –

> *Mr. D's goal was to help his child get his homework finished in less than two hours a night. He thought about how he could use the Standard Strategies and this is what he decided. He could use the 'Process not Product' strategy to compliment his child's efforts to get his work finished and the 'Whose Problem is it?' strategy to tell him of the consequences of not doing this. He could use the 'Failure as Learning Opportunity' strategy to talk to his son about why he wasn't getting work finished on time and to find possible ways to make this happen. The 'Brownie Points' strategy could be used to compliment his son whenever he finished work on time.*
>
> *He thought that his son's not finishing work was more to do with lack of understanding of what he had to do rather than deliberately wasting time so he decided to use the 'Failure as a Learning Opportunity' strategy to help his son understand what he had to do.*
>
> *Mrs. Y wanted her son to get better grades in all of his subjects! She thought he was not working hard enough. She could use the 'Process not Product' strategy to remind him about what he did when he got a good grade for his work or the 'Whose Problem is it?' strategy to make sure he understood the consequences of getting low grades. She might use the 'Failure as Learning Opportunity' strategy to talk about why he wasn't getting the grades he was capable of getting and the 'Brownie Points' strategy to compliment him whenever his grades improved.*
>
> *Mrs. Y decided to use the 'Process not Product' strategy to take the pressure off her son's efforts to get good grades while encouraging him to do everything he could to improve his results.*
>
> *Ms. P's daughter thought she was stupid and she had lost confidence in her ability to learn. Ms. P looked over the strategies and came up with these ideas of how to use them. She could use the 'Process not Product' strategy to tell her daughter what she was doing well and that her work would improve if she continued to do those things. She could use the 'Whose Problem is it?' strategy to help her daughter understand that she was there to help her when she needed support. She decided against*

*using the 'Failure as Learning Opportunity' strategy because she did not want to emphasize the idea of failure and she could use the 'Brownie Points' strategy to reward her daughter every time she did something well, no matter how small.*

*Ms. P was so worried about her daughter that she used several of these strategies and helped her partner learn how to use them too.*

As you can see it only takes a small step to make these strategies work for any learning goal.

Take your chosen Standard Strategy and convert it into a strategy that helps your child move to the learning goal you have set. Add this to Step 4 of your child's Ultimate Success Formula.

**2.** How to adjust Super Strategies to Success Strategies

Take the Super Strategy you have chosen and turn it into a Success Strategy by linking it to your learning goal.

Here are some examples.

*Mr. F wanted to make sure his son understood the math he was learning in class. His discovered his son needed help to Make School Make Sense and chose the Super Strategy of 'Matching' support to learning preferences. Results from the Porter Diagnostic Assessment at Vnaya. com showed that his son was a Picture Smart learner.*

*Mr. F's Success Strategy was to use diagrams and pictures when helping his son with math homework. Mr. F, a Word Smart learner, would not have used this Success Strategy if he had not discovered his son's preferred learning style.*

*Mrs. R wanted to help her son do well in an upcoming geography examination. The results of the checklist in Step 2 showed that her son did not need support to Learn how to Learn or to Make School Make sense but did need support Move to Mastery and to catch up on learning he had missed.*

*She decided to discover what support was available for her son who was a Number Smart learner. After looking at the support that was available she decided to hire an on-line tutor who taught geography and who was also a Number Smart learner.*

*Mrs. S was tired of trying to get her daughter out of bed each morning to go to school. She knew that when her daughter got to school she was too tired to learn well. Mrs. S's goal was to make sure her daughter got enough sleep so she had the energy she needed to be able to learn. She chose the Super Strategy of asking questions to help her daughter think about going to bed on time. Each night she would ask her daughter - What time are you thinking of going to bed? What might stop you going to bed at that time? Is there anything I could do to make it easier for you to get to bed on time? The questions helped her daughter understand the importance of getting enough sleep and eased her into earlier bedtimes.*

Now you try - choose a Super Strategy from the section that relates to your child's learning need and think of a way to link it to the learning goal you have set. You don't have to get this right the first time!

Add this strategy to Step 3 of your child's Ultimate Success Formula

**3.** How to adapt Specific Strategies to Success Strategies

There are over a hundred Success Strategies to choose from and within the scope of this book it is impossible to show you how to link every strategy to every learning goal and learning preference. Use the same process you used before to link your chosen Success Strategy to your learning goal and your child's preferred way of learning.

There are examples of completed Ultimate Success Formulae at the end of section 3 of this book that will help with this process.

Now you have three Success Strategies you can start to use immediately. Using three strategies that work is going to make an enormous difference to your child's learning and will take away the stress and exhaustion you feel when using strategies that don't work.

This process takes a little imagination and some creativity. If you need help on how to complete this step contact me at patricia@leadingtolearning.com

There is one more part to this step of the Porter Process. You need to decide when and how you are going to use these Success Strategies. Can you use them everyday or only on certain days? Could they be used when your child is doing homework or when everyone is around the dinner table? Do you use them when your child is working on a certain subject or can you use them whatever work your child is doing?

Who else needs to know about these strategies so they can help you use them with your child? Teacher? Spouse? Sibling? Friend?

How will you share this information? Talk to them? Show them your child's Journey to Success? Ask them to describe how they would use the strategies?

And most importantly, what is the first thing you will do now you have this information? What is the first action you will take to put these strategies into place? That is something only you can decide. Use the Plan of Action worksheet to help you decide exactly how you are going to use these strategies. Keep the completed worksheet where everyone can refer to it easily.

# Strategies for Success

## 1. Standard Strategy to Success Strategy
Standard Strategy chosen


Learning goal


**Success Strategy**  (link learning goal and Standard Strategy)



## 2. Super Strategy to Success Strategy
Super Strategy chosen


Learning goal


**Success Strategy**  (link learning goal and Super Strategy)



## 3. Specific Strategy to Success Strategy
Specific Strategy chosen


Learning goal


Success strategy (link learning goal with specific strategy)

# Plan of action

## 1. When will you use these strategies?

## 2. Who will help you?

## 3. Who will you share this information with?

## 4. What action will you take first?

# Step 5 –

# Go further

'Every new beginning comes from some other beginning's end.'
Seneca

---

| **Step 5    Celebrate Success** |
| **Review and renew** |

---

## What you will learn

- That success needs a celebration

- To review what worked well

- To renew the process

## Why this information is important

- Learning is a continual process; there are always more goals to reach. It is important to know when one goal has been achieved and to set the next

## What you will do

- Celebrate arriving at your destination

- Review how you got there

- Decide on the next destination

Now you are using the strategies that lead to success you will notice the changes that are taking place in your child's learning. Do not expect all your results to be positive, especially when you first start to use the strategies you have chosen. For instance now you are using only the strategies that lead to success you might think that you are not doing enough to help your child or your child might think you are not giving him or her enough support. Take time to explain to your child what you are doing and why you are doing it. It may take a little while for both you and your child to settle in to this new way of working.

Keeping a progress report is a good way to remember what you did that worked well and what you did that didn't produce the results you wanted. Use the worksheet at the end of this step to note what you did and what happened as a result. Use these notes to help you review what you have been doing and to refine how you work with your child.

What did you think of the strategies you used? What part worked best for you? Was there some part of the strategy that you considered changing, tweaking in some way? Did doing that make things easier?

Every child is different and reacts differently to the same strategy. Every parent has a slightly different way of using strategies and therefore gets slightly different results. Think about how you could tweak the strategies you are using to make them even more beneficial.

Your crystal clear learning goal included some form of measurement of success. You might have defined success as getting better grades or improving learning behavior but whatever you chose as your learning goal be prepared to recognize, and accept when it has been reached.

Then celebrate your successes. This celebration can be as easy as saying 'well done!' to your child or as hard as organizing a special treat of some kind. Don't forget to tell *yourself* how well you have done, as well as your child. This is a team success! Celebrating success gives an ending to one journey and opens up the possibility of the next.

This is when you start the process again because you set a new learning goal. It is easier and quicker to do than the first time because you have gone through the process once and know how to take the 5 steps.

# Summary

When you have achieved the goal you set it is time to make another one.

# Progress report

1. What worked best

2. What I need to tweak

3. Next steps

# In conclusion...

Congratulations! You have created your child's Ultimate Success Formula, worked out how to use it and started your child's on his or her journey to success. How quickly your child gets to the destination depends on what goal you have set and the strategies you have chosen. I have seen amazing differences happen in as little as two weeks but I know that sometimes real, lasting change can take longer.

However long you and your child take to complete your journey you know that you are moving in the right direction, you are leading your child to learning.

Now you have access to a way of helping your child learn that you can use over and over again as often as you need to. You can increase your child's ability to learn. You can help your child succeed in school.

These 5 steps may be all you need to lead your child to learning but if you need more guidance or support you can access more help from –

patricia@leadingtolearning.com to schedule a free 20 minute call about any concerns you may have.

www.Vnaya.com where specially trained Learning Leaders at ready to guide you through the Porter Process.

# Section 3:

# Strategies

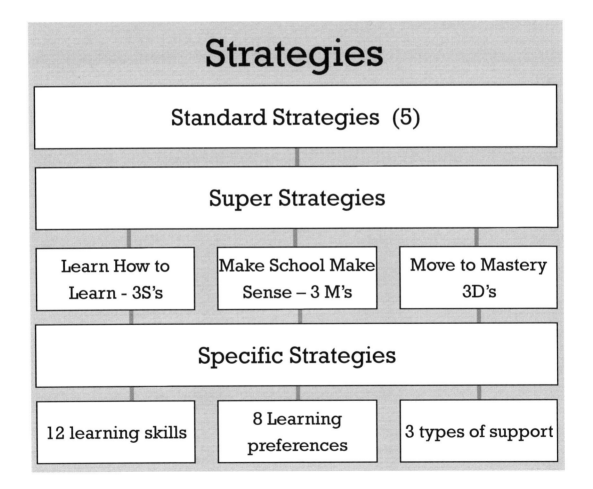

**Strategies**

Standard Strategies  (5)

Super Strategies

| Learn How to Learn - 3S's | Make School Make Sense – 3 M's | Move to Mastery 3D's |

Specific Strategies

| 12 learning skills | 8 Learning preferences | 3 types of support |

Welcome to the third section of the book where you will discover the strategies that will lead to school success. You will find three types of strategies in this section.

- Standard strategies - five general strategies that everyone can use

- Super Strategies – three for each stage of learning, learning how to learn, making school make sense and moving to mastery.

- Specific Strategies – for each learning skill, each learning preference and method of providing extra support

The first set– **Standard Strategies** – are general strategies that encourage good learning.

The second set - **Super Strategies** – relate to the three areas of learning need.

The third set - **Specific Strategies** –  relate to the development of specific skills, adaptations to learning styles and choice and provision of extra support.

You will not need all these strategies. Look at the section that relates to your child's specific learning need and choose the strategies that will work for you.

Then change these strategies into **Success Strategies** and start making a difference in your child's learning life.

This section ends with examples of what your child's **Ultimate Success Formula** might look like.

# Standard Strategies

I'm going to suggest the following five standard strategies:

- Look for the good

- Praise the process not the product

- Whose problem is it?

- See failures as learning opportunities

- Brownie points

These five strategies work with all children, they are easy to implement and to fit into your daily routine, and they will have a positive effect on a child's attitude to learning. Many parents are already using these strategies but they are so important it is worth repeating them. Read them all and decide which one you will start to use with your child. When you are happy with using that strategy add one of the others until you are using all 5 standard strategies.

## Look for the Good

All too often a parent will focus on what a child cannot do and ignore the things students can do. No one likes to be reminded that what they did was wrong. Everyone likes to be told what he or she did that was right. When you are told you did something well you will strive to repeat what you did and to make it even better. It is the same with children. If a child was struggling to do his work and had lost the motivation to continue trying rather than tell the child that he was wasting time I would find something he was doing well and praise him for doing it. It always worked. The child would pause, then get back to doing his work.

There is always something a child is doing well.

It may be the way the child is trying to do their work, not getting upset when things go wrong, using their time well, organizing their books, or holding their pencil. It is always possible to find something good in any situation.

When you find 'the good' in a situation the level of trust between you and your child increases and he or she will try harder to make more 'good' things happen.

Even when you have to make a negative comment it is best to start by saying something positive. For instance - instead of saying, "When are you going to start your homework?"

you could say, "Looks like you've got a bit of homework to do. Shouldn't take long, then you can watch TV or go on the computer. It will take a little practice to get into the habit of using this strategy but it is well worth the effort.

## Praise the Process not Product

Students need praise for what they do but if you only praise the product - the work your child has done – he or she will never really understand and appreciate the effort it took. Always acknowledge a good piece of work but give praise for the process your child went through. By doing this you are encouraging your child to use the same process again and reinforcing the belief that effort pays off.

The more specific you are with your praise the more your child will understand what he or she did right and try to do it again next time. For example - after a child has finished a project and been given a good grade you may say, "I really liked the way you persevered even when it was hard to get the work done, and as a result you have a great grade, well done!"

Again, learning to praise the process takes practice.

## Whose Problem is it?

If your child has a problem doing his or her homework it is important to understand who owns the problem. The person who owns the problem is the one who has to find the solution. The problem may belong to a teacher or a child.

For instance, if your child is struggling because he has not brought the textbooks he needs or because he has left it too late to complete the work the problem belongs to him. His lack of action was the cause of the problem and it is up to him to find a solution.

Alternatively it might be that your child doesn't understand the homework instructions or how to do the work he has been set. In that case the problem belongs to the teacher who has not made it clear to the student what he or she has to do.

In the first instance, when the problem belongs to your child, you may help your child set up a system so he remembers which books he needs or when homework is due but you should not run around finding the books he needs or helping him get his work done on time. In the next section there are strategies you can use to help your child become responsible for his or her actions.

If the problem belongs to the teacher because your child has not understood what he needs to do you can help your child by contacting the teacher and explaining the situation. The teacher can then work with your child to increase his understanding.

Your role is to determine to whom the problem belongs and to encourage that person to find a solution.

Do not take on a problem that belongs to someone else! I see parents doing this all the time. They are so concerned that their child does their homework they nag them to get started and may even do some or all of the child's work just to get it done on time. This does not help the child or the teacher and it increases the stress on parent and family.

It may be difficult to ensure that the right person takes responsibility for learning issues but it is the only way to be sure that the issue can be resolved.

# See Failures as Learning Opportunities

Most of the time parents, students and even teachers see failures such as not being able to do something or getting a poor mark on an assignment or a test as a judgment on a student's performance. And it is. But it is also much more, it is an indication that the student needs to learn something. It should be seen as a learning opportunity.

In my class, much to the consternation of my students, I never let them use erasers. Not because I expected their work to be perfect, just the opposite. I needed to see their mistakes so I knew what they needed to learn. Mistakes were seen as a learning opportunity.

When your child makes mistakes or fails to achieve a certain goal, use that failure to point out what he or she needs to learn so that results could be better next time.

# Brownie Points

Everyone needs Brownie Points. They are often difficult to get and are very easily and quickly lost.

A 'Brownie Point' is something that makes you feel good. It can be a positive comment ('I like your shirt'), a checkmark on an assignment, a smile, a helping hand, a good deed, anything that makes the recipient feel valued and respected.

Students (and, I suspect, everyone else) need at least ten Brownie Points each day to maintain good attitudes and a sense of progress. More than ten are needed for real progress to take place! You are the first and main source of Brownie Points for your child with teachers, friends and other family members coming in a close second.

It is not difficult to give a child Brownie Points but it is incredibly easy to help a child lose the ones he or she has. One negative remark or one sideways glance wipes out ten Brownie Points in a moment and a child's attitude may be changed for the worst.

Try to follow these guidelines –

1. Always find something good to praise
2. Before you say anything vaguely negative to your child remember to say one good thing first.
3. Try to turn the negative comment into something positive.

For example, when you want to tell your child that he has done poor work you might say "I know that you can do excellent work, I have seen what you can do and I have been impressed by it, but I am wondering why this work is not your best, perhaps you need help"?

Brownie Points are a powerful tool to help develop self-confidence and self-esteem, two of the foundational learning skills all children need.

These 5 Standard Strategies, Look for the good, Praise the process not the product, Whose problem is it? See failures as learning opportunities, and Brownie points are the basic strategies that help you lead your child to learning. They are easy to implement and fun to use and can quickly become part of your everyday interaction with your child.

# Super Strategies

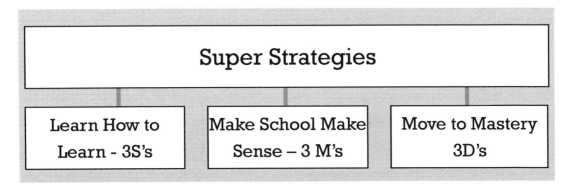

These three sets of **Super Strategies** each relate to the three stages of areas of learning need.

If your child needs support to help him or her **Learn How to Learn** look at the three Super Strategies for the first stage of learning. These strategies begin with the letter 'S'.

If your child needs support to help him or her **Make School Make Sense** look at the three Super strategies for the second stage of learning. These strategies begin with the letter 'M'.

If your child needs support to **Move to Mastery** look at the three Super strategies for the third stage of learning. These strategies begin with the letter 'D'.

The Standard Strategy you chose can be used with all children, no matter what their learning need. Super Strategies can be used to help with the three main learning needs. For instance, choose one of the three strategies Show, Share, Say if your child needs help to learn how to learn.

# Super Strategies for 'Learn How to Learn'

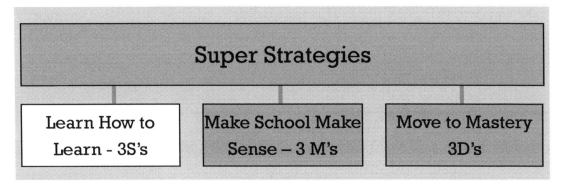

The learning strategies for this stage of learning are **3S's – Show, Share, Say©**

## Show the behavior you want to see

### The Power of Modeling

Your child loves you and wants to be like you. He or she watches and listens to everything you do even when you are not aware of it. You act as a model for your child. This means you have to be careful about what you say and do when your child is with you. But you can also use modeling to help your child learn things you want him or her to learn and do things you want him or her to do.

For instance, if you want your child to read he should see you reading. If you want your child to pay attention she should see you paying attention. If you want your child to cross the road safely he should see you taking care crossing the road.

It is easy to see how modeling works for young children but it is also a powerful tool to use with older children. If you want your child to recognize the importance of school you need to keep in contact with your child's teachers. If you want your child to avoid bad company you could talk about how you avoided this. If you want your child to learn to read he or she should see you reading and if you want your child to enjoy learning he or she should see you enjoying learning.

Never underestimate the power of modeling.

### 'Self Talk'

*Self-talk* is a way to show your thinking and help children begin to understand the processes that you take for granted but they need to learn. Self-talk is powerful because it can be used to help children learn a variety of skills.

### What is Self-talk?

'Self-talk' is when you talk to yourself within earshot of your child. It is a way of making your thought processes accessible to your child. It is not about talking directly to your child or asking him or her to listen to what you are saying. That doesn't work. You may not even be aware that your child is listening, and sometimes he or she may not be, but soon your child will be so curious about what you are doing that he or she will pay attention.

### How can I use Self-talk?

You need to set your intention to use this strategy. You need to be sure what you want your child to learn. Only then can you use self-talk in a way that will help your child develop the skill he or she needs to develop.

For instance, if a child needs to learn how to pay attention you could talk about how you need to look carefully at something so you know what to do.

Here is an example.

Mom: - 'I need to go shopping. Mmmm …I wonder what I need to buy?  I will have a look in the cupboard to see what is there. (Looks in cupboard)  Oh, I can see the cereal so I don't need to buy that, and I can see sugar too so that doesn't need to go on the list?  What is missing?  I know, I can't see any cookies. I had better look for them when I go to the store."

This *self-talk* might seem a bit stilted but it is helping your child understand the need to pay attention and gather information.

Self-talk can seem strange at first but with practice you will understand how easy it is to use and how powerful it can be in helping your child develop learning skills

# Share your skills

You have many skills that you can share with your child. You have a lifetime of experiences that your child needs to know about. This 'cultural capital' consists of the skills you have built up during your life, skills such as working with others, keeping a household together, planning celebrations etc. When you include your child in these activities he or she will learn the skills that make them happen.  These are skills that can help them in their lives.

When I was young my mother taught me to how to knit. When I was in college I was short of money and I used this skill to make clothes for others that I sold to help with my finances!  The skill she had taught when I was young became a lifesaver when I was older.

## I, we, you

This is a three-step process that helps you demonstrate your skills and helps you pass them onto your child.

First you need to show your child what to do. This is the 'I' part of the title.

This step is where you do what you want your child to do while your child is watching and listening. You model what your child needs to do to get a task completed. You make this modeling clear and allow the child to question your every move.

For a young child this could be showing him or her how to tidy his of her room or how to complete a worksheet.

For an older student it might be how to structure an essay or use key words to look up information (but they will probably be better than you at this!)

The idea is to show a student all the steps that are necessary in getting something done.

Then you help your child do the task. This is the 'We' part of the title.

Now you redo the same task - or one that is very similar – with your child helping when needed but allowing him or her to do the part of the task they feel competent to complete. This step might have to be repeated several times until you are sure your child knows what to do and can do it on his or her own.

The last step is "You". This is when you check that your child has learned what to do. You stand by ready to offer help while your child completes the task. Be generous with praise.

Now that you are both sure that the child can complete the task he can be made responsible for doing this again in the future.

# Say - words that help your child think.

## The power of words

Whatever you say to your child either helps or hinders your child's thinking skills. Words are never neutral. Whenever you speak to your child in a way that shuts down thinking such as when you ask a yes or no question you are missing an opportunity to help your child learn.

Not everything you say to your child should be directed at helping your child think. Sometimes you just want to communicate instructions or warnings. But if you are aware of how your language is affecting your child's thinking you may be able to find more times to use the kind of language that does this.

Language that stops learning is 'closed' and requires no response or a one-word response. For instance "Don't do that!" does not require a response and "Do you want to do that?" requires only a yes or no answer.

Language that encourages learning is called "open" and requires the person to think about his or her response. For instance "Why shouldn't you do that?" means the child has to think about his or her reasons. And "Why do you want to do that?" also requires the child to think.

Subtle changes in how you use language can have enormous impact on how well your child thinks.

## Ask the right questions

One way to use language is to ask questions that encourage thinking. But knowing what questions to ask can be difficult. Here are some questions you can use when you are helping with homework.

- How will you do that?

- How can we find out?

- What do you think the problem is?

- Can we make a plan so we don't miss anything?

Use these when your child is doing homework as a way of helping him or her think about what needs doing

- How is it different from/ like ___?

- How could you do it differently?

- How have you done this before?

- What do you need to do next?

- What do you think will happen if_____?

- Can you think of a better way to do this?

Use these when your child has completed work and you want him or her to think about what has been done

- How do you know it is right?

- How do you feel when….

- Why did you do it that way?

- Yes that is right, how do you know it is right?

Choose a couple of these questions, ones that you feel happy using, and try using them with your child. Remember to listen to the answer!

There are many ways of using this type of question. Use these to help your child think about how to do homework.

# Super Strategies for Making School Make Sense

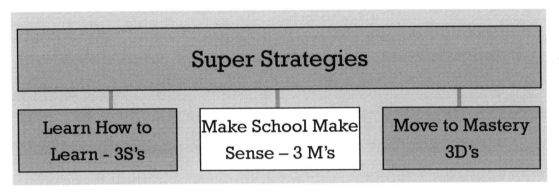

The learning strategies for this stage of learning are - **3M's – Meet, Match, Mentor**

## Meet your child's teacher

Home/school links are very important. Parents and teachers need to communicate and share concerns and ideas about how a child's education. This communication can prevent students falling through the gap between home and school. But meeting and talking to your child's teacher can be a struggle. Finding mutually acceptable times can be difficult and even when parents and teachers meet, language can be a problem. Teachers often use 'teacher talk' and this can be confusing for parents. Despite these issues it is important to open lines of communication.

### Parent/teacher meetings

There are formal and informal ways to make these meetings happen. The formal ways include the regular parent/teacher meetings that schools set up as well as report cards and participation in Parent Advisory Committees. Where I live any parent who has a child in school is automatically a member of their school's Parent Advisory Committee and can attend their meetings.

The informal ways to meet teachers include volunteering in the school or at special events and setting up a time to talk to the teacher outside the formal meeting times mentioned above.

Teachers are busy people. If you want to meet your child's teacher it is wise to phone first to set up a meeting and to do your homework before you meet the teacher. Here is a list of things to consider before the meeting.

i.   Be clear about the information you either want from the teacher or want to share with the teacher. You could mention why you want the meeting when you schedule it.

ii.  Think about what you want to say or to ask. Then put your thoughts in a written list. Schools can be intimidating places for those not used to being in them and even the best intentions get lost when you have to squeeze into a desk or onto a kindergarten size chair!

iii. Refer to this list when you are talking to the teacher and take time to get your thoughts across and to listen to the teacher's response. If you need or want to set up another meeting say so and set it up before you leave.

Meeting with and talking to your child's teacher will resolve most of your concerns. However, if you still have concerns you can ask to see the Principal or take the concerns to your parent representative. Both these people will know how you can take your concerns to a higher authority if you need to.

# Match support to how your child likes to learn

Children learn in different ways. Some children are Word Smart and prefer to learn by talking, reading and writing. Others are Picture Smart and prefer to learn by being shown what to do and using diagrams and flow charts. Still others are Body Smart and learn best when moving, or Number Smart and prefer a logical structured approach to learning. A few children are primarily Nature or Music Smart. Some children learn best when they can bounce ideas off others (People Smart) and some prefer to work things out on their own (Self Smart).

The free assessment at www.Vnaya.com will help you discover how your child likes to learn and you can find descriptions of preferred learning styles at http://www.vnaya.com/eonline/users/learning_styles

When you match the support you give to how your child likes to learn you will find that your support is more easily understood and accepted and your child will enjoy learning more.

The way you learn may be different from the way your child learns. Do not assume your child learns the same way you do and needs the same kind of support you needed. I have met parents who were Word Smart learners trying to tell their child how to do something, when the child, a Picture Smart learner, needed to be *shown* what to do. This resulted in frustration for the parent and confusion for the child.

# Mentor - guide your child through the system

Children will meet many challenges during the years that they are part of a school system. They may have trouble making friends, getting used to a new teacher, deciding which courses to take, knowing what to do when they are unhappy in school. They need you to guide them through these years and to help them get the education they need and deserve. There are two ways you can do this.

## Share your experiences of school and learning

By sharing your experience of schooling and of learning you can help your child understand that you too had good times and bad times and give your child some ideas about how to handle the ups and downs of his or her school career. Perhaps your child is going through similar situations and knowing what worked – or didn't – for you could help him decide what would work for him.

## Become an advocate for your child

Part of your mentoring role is to be come an advocate for your child and to ensure your child takes advantage of all that schools can offer. To do this well you need to know what is happening in your child's school (see meet the teacher above) and what is available in your school district. A way of learning about this is to explore the district website, a rich source of all kinds of information, and to join your school's parent association. By joining the parent association in your school you may be able to influence aspects of your child's learning and make the school a better place for all students.

Your role as a mentor will change as your child moves from Elementary school to High school and beyond but the guidance you give your child will always be needed and will help your child understand the importance you place on his or her education.

# Super Strategies for Move to Mastery

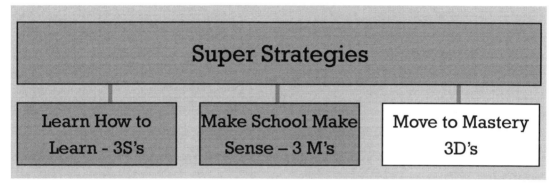

The learning strategies for this stage of learning are the **3D's - Discover, Decide, Deliver**

## Discover what support is available

This is the first step in providing support that helps your child Move to Mastery. You may already know of tutors and tutoring services in your area as many of them are advertised in the media or through the informal parent networks in schools. However it is a good idea to search for other options. You can use Google to find on-line tutoring services if you decide to go that route or connect to the local parenting group to learn about nearby options. Whatever you decide to do take time to make sure that the tutoring will meet your child's needs. Ask for references and guarantees.

You could also check to see if your child's school offers after school support such as homework clubs or extra programs. These can be very useful as they create a continuum of support for your child.

Are there any books and educational resources that your child could use? The school may be able to offer advice and you may be able to buy a copy of the textbooks they use. This can be very useful when helping with homework or using a tutor to review schoolwork.

You may wish to use the services of a learning specialist, someone who can give you information about your child's learning. Schools have access to Educational Psychologists but thy usually have long waiting lists and work mainly with children with severe learning difficulties. There are educational psychologists who work privately and who may be able to offer the support you need but they can be expensive and I have worked with several parents who took this route and were dissatisfied with the report they got.

Make a list of all your options before you decide on the type of support that will make the difference you want to see in your child.

# Decide who will offer support

The main sources for support in this stage of learning are you, the school and tutors. Each has their strengths and weaknesses and you may wish to mix and match all three types.

## a. You

The benefits of you providing support come from the close relationship you have with your child. You know better than anyone your child's feelings and attitudes towards their work. You will know when your child is struggling to learn and can adjust support to meet your child's needs.

If you are going to offer support by helping with homework, providing resources, or sharing a skill you have, you need to be able to separate your role as teacher and your role as parent.

Some parents may opt to home-school their child. This approach can be successful, but it can be stressful, and it does require the parent to be able to access resources and spend many hours helping their children learn.

If you decide that you will be the main source of support for your child's learning the Learning Leaders at www.Vnaya.com are always ready to provide you with any guidance and support you may need.

## b. The school

You may decide that your child could benefit from extra support from school. You could discuss your child's needs with his or her teacher and negotiate for what your child needs. This might be as simple as being placed closer to the front of the class to accommodate vision or hearing difficulties or asking that your child be placed in a group where he or she could get extra help. If you already have a relationship with your child's teacher (see Meet the teacher above) this is easier to do.

## c. Tutors

Many parents decide that their child needs extra support from a tutor or a tutoring program either because they do not have the time or the skill to provide the help their child needs. Tutoring can be an excellent way of providing support to Move to Mastery. However there are some actions you need to take to ensure you get the kind of tutoring that is right for your child. You can read about these in the Success Strategies part of the book that follows this section.

# Deliver – what works for you

How are you going to deliver the support your child needs? Providing support is quite a commitment and you need to be sure that it does not impinge too much on the way you live your life. If providing support takes too much time or is too expensive your child will feel this pressure and your relationship will suffer. You also need to be sure that by offering support to one child you are not depriving another. The benefits and barriers of different support delivery systems are described below.

## a. You

The benefits of providing the support yourself include cost, flexibility and awareness.

- The cost of you providing support may be negligible but do consider whether you can afford to spend the time to do this. The important point to consider is that learning support needs to be provided on a regular and consistent basis, so be sure that you can manage this as well as other responsibilities

- Because you will be working at home you can schedule support at any time that suits you and your child. You can also be flexible about the type of support you offer, changing content or approach as needed.

- You know your child better than anyone else. You will be aware of your child's moods and reactions. Children at certain stages of their life are more likely to accept teaching from someone other than family members

- I urge you not to continue providing support that threatens the special relationship you have with your child. Your relationship is too important to be put under stress.

The barriers of providing support include time, availability, expertise and resources.

- You may not have the time to commit to helping your child on a regular basis and your work may mean that you are unavailable to provide help when your child needs it.

- Do you have the subject expertise that is required or the teaching skills you may need?

- Access to suitable resources such as textbooks and reference books is important. Schools may let you borrow the books you need and the Internet could be where you go to find information. Do you have access to these?

## b. School

The benefits of asking schools to deliver support include building a relationship between home and school, access to resources and trained teachers, cost and time savings.

- If you want the school to deliver support for your child, first meet your child's teacher and see what support might be available. The school may have an after-school homework club or even a special group that would suit your child's needs. Always call first to make an appointment and be prepared to meet the teacher during or shortly after the school day.

- The school will have ready access to the books your child needs and this extra support may come at no cost. Trained teachers whom your child already knows will run classes and extra lessons.

- Your child is already in school so you will not have to spend as much time helping your child.

Barriers to school support include lack of finance which limits the provision of extra resources, inability or unwillingness of staff to work extra hours, lack of understanding of a child's learning needs.

## c. Tutors

If you want a tutor for your child you have three options – hire a personal tutor, enroll your child in a tutoring program, use an on-line tutoring service. There are benefits and barriers to each choice.

### i. Personal tutors

The benefits of personal tutoring include flexibility, easy communication and immediate feedback.

- A personal tutor may come to your house saving you time and inconvenience. He or she will be able to create a program that meets your child's specific needs and speed of learning.

- You will have easy access to the tutor and be able to get immediate feedback about your child's progress. You will also be able to tell the tutor about any circumstances at home that may impact learning.

The barriers to this form of tutoring include cost, difficulty of finding the best tutor, and possibly limited resources.

- One-on-one tutoring can be expensive. Consider the amount of time your child might need this support and decide if the cost will work for you.

- Finding the right tutor, someone who knows how your child likes to learn, knows the content they will be teaching and has the ability to teach well is not an easy task. A tutor that works for your friend's child might not work for yours.

- Tutors are often expected to provide the resources they use. If a tutor does not have easy access to arrange of resources this could limit what he or she teaches.

## ii. Group tutoring

The benefits of group tutoring include cost, systems, resources, known teaching approach and guarantees

- It may be less expensive to enroll your child in a group program than to hire a personal tutor. (Although some of these group programs can also be quite expensive).

- Your child will become part of a system that should include regular feedback and assessment as well as systems for easy payment and communication.

- Group programs have ready access to the resources they need for the programs they deliver.

- Each group program has its own approach to teaching. You can check if this approach meets your child's learning needs before you sign up.

- These programs usually provide guarantees. However do check what is guaranteed as it may not be what you need.

The barriers to using this type of tutoring include lack of flexibility and concerns about expertise of teachers.

- You have to take your child to the program at a set time, the programs are set and can only be individualized to a certain extent, programs are of a set length and you may have to pay for a full year whether or not your child needs this amount of support.

- Many group programs employ young inexperienced teachers and rely on the program structure to deliver quality. Check on this before signing up.

## iii. Online tutoring

The benefits of on-line tutoring include flexibility, access to many expert tutors, communication, trial periods, guarantees, and convenience.

- Schedules can suit you and your child and tutoring takes place in your home. There is no time lost in travel to and from tutoring. Programs can be individualized as needed and tutors can either work from the curriculum or to a child's personal needs. Payment can be for a few weeks or a few months. Your child may be able to take more than one lesson a week.

- On-line tutoring services employ a range of tutors with qualifications in different subject areas. This makes it easy to find the kind of tutor your child needs.

- Communication is as easy as using the telephone, e-mail or a specialized online technology system the service has set up specifically for parents.

- Some on-line services allow you a trial period to make sure the service is what your child needs. This may come at no cost.

- Most on-line services offer a guarantee – check out the terms.

- All tutoring is done in your own home, at your own time and at a cost that is much less than personal tutoring. Students will have their own tutor (see benefits of personal tutoring above) at a much lower cost.

Barriers to on-line tutoring are age of child, access to technology and limited hands on experiences.

- I would not recommend on-line tutoring for a very young child. Children younger than 5 need to build a close personal relationship with a tutor and would probably benefit more from face-to-face tutoring.

- Your child needs the relevant technological skills to use this type of tutoring.

There are many decisions to make and many opportunities to do the wrong thing for the right reason. If you are not completely sure what type of help your child needs you can get advice from the Learning Leaders at www.Vnaya.com.

# Specific Strategies

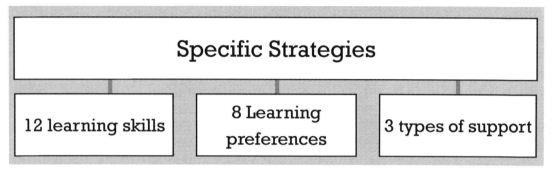

Specific Strategies relate to a child's specific learning needs at each stage of the learning process.

In this section you will be provided with over a hundred Success Strategies you can learn about and use. Not every strategy will appeal to you but there are enough for you to choose ones that do. In the first part of this section, I will advise on how to choose the strategies most appropriate to your child's learning needs.

If you have already taken the free diagnostic learning assessment at www.Vnaya.com you will know the stage of learning in which your child needs support and the specific type of support within that stage that he or she needs. (If you have not already done this, now would be a good time.)

For instance, if your child needs support at the first stage of learning – learning how to learn – the results of the assessment will have told you what skills your child needs to develop and you will be ready to look at that section of the Success Strategies listed below and choose which strategies you will use.

If your child needs support at the second stage of learning - to make school make sense – you will have learned how your child prefers to learn and can go to the section where there are strategies you can use with your child.

If your child needs support to Move to Mastery you can look at the last section of these Success Strategies and choose which you will use.

Please take the time to glance through the strategies in other sections even if you are not going to use them. They will help you understand the differences between the skills and learning preferences and will reinforce the importance of not guessing what support your child needs.

You may also want to help your child develop more than one learning skill or to use strategies that relate to more than one learning preference. In that case look through the strategies in each of the sections before deciding which to use.

# Specific Strategies for 'Learn how to learn'

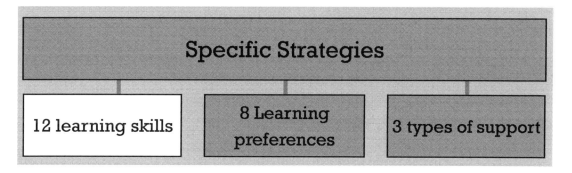

There are twelve foundational learning skills that children need to develop to be successful in school. In creating this list I draw on the findings of Dr. R. Feuerstein and Dr. M.L. Jensen and I have adapted and modified their findings to make them of use to parents who want to help children succeed in school.

## Learn How to Learn - Foundational learning skills

1. *Physical learning skills*
   *Vision*
   *Hearing*
   *Movement*
   *Energy*

2. *Emotional learning skills*
   *Attitudes about -*
       *Themselves*
       *Others*
       *Their work*
       *The future*

3. *Cognitive Learning Skills*
   *Attention*
   *Understanding*
   *Processing*
   *Production*

There are three groups of learning skills. The first group contains the physical skills that children need to be able to get started on learning, the second group contains the emotional attitudes that enable children to be ready to learn and the third group contains the cognitive skills that children need to do schoolwork.

For a detailed description of these learning skills and why they are important go to http://www.vnaya.com/eonline/users/learning_skills

If your child needs to develop several learning skills start with the ones in the first group – the physical learning skills. Only when your child has the skills that make him or her able to learn can you begin to develop other learning skills.

# Physical learning skills

Vision, hearing, movement and energy are the skills that ensure a child is physically able to learn. They are also the skills that are often overlooked when thinking about learning problems. For instance I have worked with students aged 11 and 12 who were struggling to learn because no one had understood how the frequent colds they had when they were young had led to intermittent hearing loss that meant they had missed much of what they were being taught. Vision problems can also go unnoticed because children cannot tell you what they can't see!

These physical skills are 'ground zero' for learning. Without these skills your child never gets started.  Fortunately once recognized they are easy to develop.

### Vision

Lack of good vision leads to inability to read well, see the blackboard, understand information, or move easily. Poor visual perception leads to lack of understanding, poor attention and loss of confidence.

If your child has problems with his or her vision (results from learning assessment at www. Vnaya.com), or if you suspect your child has problems, it is important to have his or her eyesight checked by a professional.  Be aware that as a child grows his or her eyesight can change. I suggest an annual eyesight test for your child.

### Hearing

The inability to hear clearly prevents a child from getting information he or she needs, lack of understanding, poor attention, poor language development and difficulty making friends. Hearing loss is common and can be very difficult to diagnose as children develop coping techniques that hide the issue.

If results of the skill assessment show your child may have hearing issues I suggest you have his or her hearing checked by a professional. Your child may have had hearing loss in the past that has had an effect on learning. If your child suffered from frequent colds when young he or she might have missed some important lessons and, without that background context for learning, be struggling to make sense of what he or she is being taught.

*Strategies to help overcome hearing loss*
- Be aware of the possibility of intermittent hearing loss and its effect on other learning skills

- Make sure your child is looking at you when you speak

- Inform the school of this issue and ask what accommodations they can make

- Remind your child to ask you to repeat what you have said when he or she has not heard properly

- Ask your child to repeat what you have told him so you are sure he has heard correctly

# Movement
The ability to move easily and gracefully is developmental. No one expects a three year-old to run and jump as well as a twelve year-old and some children are naturally more agile than others. However, when a child goes to school he or she will be expected to move around the classroom with care and to be able to hold a pencil or pen to form letters and numbers.

A child with poor movement will be clumsy, have poor handwriting, and difficulty seeing spatial relationships. Lack of this skill limits what the child is able to learn.

*Strategies that develop movement*
- If you think your child is late developing these skills I suggest you check his or her developmental level against the norms for children of that age.

- Talk to a physiotherapist about specific activities that can help your child

- Use suitable activities to develop both gross and fine motor skills (sports, playing cards, etc.)

- Provide advice on how to avoid being clumsy such as taking your time when moving, looking carefully at where you want to go.

# Energy
Children need to be able to use their body and brain in ways that are needed for learning. Learning takes energy. Without energy a child's brain cannot work. We all know the feeing that we can't think straight because we are either tired or hungry and that our behaviour is affected as a result. A child who lacks energy will not be able to learn.

Lack of energy is caused by poor nutrition, illness, lack of sleep, and too many after-school activities. Children who lack energy will be sleepy, unable to think or pay attention, unmotivated and may even be badly behaved.

*Strategies that ensure a child has energy to learn*

- Check your child has breakfast and is provided with a snack to eat during the school day

- Check on hours of sleep each night – not just hours in bedroom. Young children need between 9 and 10 hours sleep each night, older students need a minimum of 8 hours sleep.

- Strategies for getting a child to bed include giving a ten-minute warning, a bed-time story and snack, negotiating a set time to go to bed. Avoid having to continually remind your child about bedtime. This can be annoying and unproductive.

- Consider the number of after-school activities your child is involved in and relate these to your child's age. Don't let participation in these activities take away energy needed for formal learning during school time.

- Give your child a snack and a short break before they start their homework

- Limit the amount of time your child spends doing homework. It is generally accepted that students should spend no more than ten minutes for each grade level. For instance a child in grade 5 would spend 50 minutes doing homework.

# Emotional learning skills

Emotional skills ensure that students have good attitudes about themselves, others, their work and the future.

## Attitudes about themselves

Children need to have <u>self-confidence</u> and <u>self-esteem</u> so they feel that they are able to learn

There are many strategies parents can use to build self-confidence and self-esteem:

### Brownie Points

This strategy is included in the Standard Strategy section but it is especially useful as a way to increase a child's self confidence and self esteem so I decided to include it as a Success Strategy in this section. Brownie Points work well with young children but can easily be adapted for use with older children. It is a way to reward students for doing something well

It is easy to send a child messages that suggest they are not doing as well as they should be. In class, children get these messages all the time – poor marks, comments from the teacher, reprimands about their behavior, feeling that they are never going to meet expectations etc.

A student gets many of these messages every day and they gradually erode self-confidence.

Giving a student 'Brownie Points' is a way of rewarding a student every time he or she does something well. 'Brownie Points' can be as simple as a kind word – "I like the way you did that", a hug, or a series of check marks on a chart that build up to a reward when a certain number have been collected.

The key to success when using cumulative points is for everyone to be clear how they are to be won, how many need to be won in a certain time frame and what the reward will be.

### Provide experiences that help the student feel in charge

Many students feel they have no power because they do not know how to make things happen. By giving students instructions on how to take charge of situations you are helping them feel more powerful and therefore more self-confident.

Here are some suggestions for working with a young child.

Teach the child to –

- Use the telephone

- Know how and when to call the emergency number

- Be able to give their name and full address, and when to use this information safely

- How to take messages

- How to prepare simple food

- How to ask the teacher a question

- How to write her homework agenda

- How to organize her books

- How to set a schedule

Suggestions for older students include –

- Creating a Homework checklist so the child feels in control of what has to be done

- Creating a list of the actions that lead to completion of a project

- How to ask for help in class

- Creating a schedule of upcoming event and work requirements and setting a pre-date to get the work done

- Keep a record of their successes somewhere where they can see it!

### Celebrate successes

Students who lack self-confidence do not believe in their ability to achieve anything. They might think that things go well by luck rather than by their own efforts or they might not recognize when they achieve something. You need to point out all their 'wins' so that they come to understand that they have created their own success.

For example, with a young student you could find some visible way of recording their success – stickers, chart, etc. With an older student verbal praise might be enough.

### Find something to praise

When you are upset with your child, or angry about something he has done, you might have to think carefully before you find something to praise your child for, but it can be done. Students respond to praise – as long as it is genuine – and change their behavior as a result. In class, when a child is behaving badly, not working or not producing any work that is worth praising, I have been known to compliment a child on something as trivial as the way he held his pencil!

For example, with a young child you might say that you liked the way she listened to what you said. With an older student you might acknowledge that he didn't get a good mark but that you liked how much effort he put into researching the project.

### Concentrate on one thing at a time.

When a student is struggling with schoolwork do not expect him to do well on all subjects. Initially choose one subject where they are struggling – and concentrate on helping your child feel good about his or her progress in that subject.

### List successes

Have a book in which you can record successes. Add one or more of your child's successes to it every day. The successes may be small, such remembering to bring a book home or large such as getting a great mark for a piece of work. Students may also be encouraged to Tweet their successes.

### Small steps

Help children see how well they are working by breaking big tasks into more manageable tasks and then check each off when completed.

### Identify your child's talents

What can your child do well? What does your child enjoy doing? Use those activities to compliment your child.

### Accept compliments gracefully

Give him or her the words that they can use to accept a compliment gracefully. Children may not know how to accept compliments and this leads to lack of self-esteem.

*Ask your child to help you*

This shows that you believe they can do the job and that you respect their contribution.

*Play together*

Play is a good way to develop self-confidence especially when your child can play the game better than you!

*Let your child take healthy risks*

Don't instill fear in your child. Let him or her take risks. Be sure that they are not too far beyond your child's capacity.

*Don't rescue your child*

If you jump in to solve your child's problems he or she will never gain the confidence to solve them on their own. When your child has a problem give him or her time to find a solution before you offer one.

*Have consistent rules*

Make sure your child knows what behaviour is acceptable and what the consequences are for misbehaving. Be consistent so your child has confidence in knowing what to do.

## Attitudes about others

Children need skills of <u>sharing</u> and <u>responsibility</u> so they can learn from others. Here are some of the strategies that help your child develop these skills:

*Who is responsible?*

Children need to know what you expect them to be responsible for. Make sure your child knows what you expect him to be responsible for. Responsibilities can be negotiated but having them clearly stated avoids misunderstandings.

*Have consequences*

When your child understands what his responsibilities are you need consequences for when he forgets or avoids doing them. The consequences should be related to the lack of action both in scope and type.

For example, when a child does not start homework on time his TV viewing may be curtailed. Use this process.

1. Remind your child that he needs to start homework
2. If child does not start within 5 minutes – parent reminds child again and gently reminds him/her of consequences
3. Either child starts – or consequences are put in place

NO ARGUMENTS! No discussion – you are both following previously set rules.

*Never assume*

You cannot expect your child to take responsibility for something he does not know how to do. Always make sure that your child knows what to do and can do it without stress. Not sure what you child can do? Use the 'I, We, You' strategy in the Standard Strategy section.

*Age appropriate*

Give your child responsibilities that are age appropriate. Don't expect a seven year old to take responsibility for younger siblings. Do expect him or her to tidy up toys after playing with them.

*Be a role model*

You share things, don't you? Next time you share anything make sure that your child sees you do it or that you tell your child about it later. Use Self Talk (Super Strategy) to help your child know how you shared something and how good you felt doing it.

*Give your child words to use*

Sharing means taking turns. Children may not know how to ask for their turn. Tell your child to say something like, 'May I have a turn when you have finished?' or 'Would you like a piece of my cookie?'

*Provide opportunities for your child to share*

Some things are easy to share. Help your child learn how to share using small cookies or candies. Then when it comes to sharing bigger things such as toys and games he will know what to do.

*Give praise*

Children are egocentric by nature. Help children know that sharing is a good thing to do by giving them praise whenever you see them doing it. Make sure that you notice!

*Homework buddy*

Having someone to work with can be helpful for some children. This person might be at one end of the phone.

*Deciding how your child will ask for help*

Children may find it difficult to ask for the help they need. Give your child the words that he or she can use when help is needed. Discuss with your child when he might need help and how you will provide it.

## Whose problem is this?

It is not your job to do your child's homework. It is your job to ask your child if he knows what he has to do and how he can do it and then to provide him with any resources he might need to get the work done.

If your child does not know what to do or how to do it you must tell his teacher so that the teacher can re-teach what your child does not know.

### Whose responsibility is this?

Be clear about what you want your child to take responsibility for. Make sure he knows what taking responsibility looks like – perhaps she needs a list of actions she has to take

### Set timelines

Discuss what could go wrong with this timeline and address the issues. Discuss – and agree on - consequences of not meeting timelines. Set time for checking that student has acted responsibly

### Don't accept excuses

If you have made it clear what your child is responsible for and made sure that he knows what to do and can do it there should be no excuses. If your child starts to give you excuses dismiss them and move to consequences.

## Attitude about their work

The skills children need to help them have a good attitude about their work are motivation and persistence

Strategies that help develop good work attitudes include the following:

### Be a role model

Motivation is contagious. If you are motivated about something, your child could catch your motivation and may even want to help you - although I am not sure that this will work with teenagers!

Even if your child is not particularly interested in the things that interest you and that you are motivated to do and to learn he or she will be aware that your enthusiasm for something is exciting and useful and will understand what it is like to be motivated and enthusiastic about something.

If you cannot be a the role model that your child needs then introduce him or her to others who are passionate about what they do and who may be willing to share part of their day with your child.

My youngest stepson did not really know what he wanted to do with his life. One day my husband was going to meet someone at London University had asked if he could bring his son along to learn about the research this person was doing. This professor spent half a day showing my stepson around his lab and explaining that he was trying to find a cure for a disease that was spread by the larvae of a certain insect. I don't understand exactly what he was trying to discover but I do know that after that visit my stepson decided to become a medial researcher. Now, over 20 years later, he has discovered a way to slow the process of macular degeneration.

Never underestimate the power of a good role model.

### Drop Breadcrumbs

Do you remember the children's fairy story by the brothers Grimm about Hansel and Gretel? They were two children who were taken into the forest by a wicked stepmother who used a trail of breadcrumbs to help them find their way home. Well, the story did not end well for them (the birds ate the breadcrumbs and they never found their way home) but the theory was good. By following the breadcrumbs they could have reached their target, they could have found their way out of the forest.

Often children are overwhelmed by the size of a task and don't attempt it or give up on it. You can help your child feel more competent by breaking down complex tasks into smaller parts, by putting breadcrumbs in their path. This will make the task seem more manageable.

If your child lacks motivation for a task this might be the best way to help him or her get started. Don't emphasize the endpoint of the task; just tell your child what his next step needs to be. Continue doing this until he has taken all the steps necessary to reach the goal.

### Share your stories

Children think of their parents as being perfect and want to grow up to be like them. They see you as being able to do all kinds of things that they would like to be able to do but cannot.

Sometimes I work with children who give up on trying to learn to read because they know that their parents can read and they expect that they should be able to read too. They do not understand that their parents have also had to go through the process of learning how to read. By sharing your stories about your struggles to learn you help your child understand that you have been through the process that he is going through.

### Negotiate goals

Having an agreed upon goal can be a good motivator. Jointly decide on a goal, writ it down and put it where you can both see it. A visible reminder will help you keep on track.

### Plan how to achieve them

Having a goal is fine but how are you going to get there? Help your child learn how to plan the things he has to do to get to his goal. This can be very difficult for some children to do and your child will need your help to fill in the gaps. Be flexible. Goals and plans can change.

### Use the right kind of reward

Most parents try to motivate children by promising to give them something, an ice cream, a trip to the zoo, an iPad. As the child gets older – and wiser – the stakes go up. I call it 'adding a zero'. At first you offer $1 to your child to motivate her to do something. Then the amount that works jumps to $10 or even $100! Rewarding your child becomes expensive. You get frustrated, your child demands more money. And your child does not stay motivated for long.

There is a better, much less expensive, way you can motivate your child. It is called intrinsic motivation (as opposed to extrinsic motivation where your child is motivated by what he can get out of you). Intrinsic motivation happens when you praise your child for the effort he or she has put into their work.

Best of all, it is free, and it lasts a lifetime.

### Believe in your child's ability to do things

Parents tread a fine line between letting children try things for themselves and wanting to keep them safe. Being too protective of your child sends him the message that he is incapable of doing things for himself. You need to trust your child to be able to do new things and to let him try – and possibly fail – but praise him for the effort.

You need to keep him safe but you also need to believe that he can try to do things and succeed. Children who never try and fail never learn anything. Believe in your child's ability, let them try new experiences, be there to help when they fail and help them try again.

### Stop telling your child what to do

Parents are very good at telling their children what to do. After all they have been responsible for their actions while they were very young and they tell their children how to do things so that they learn the right way to do them. If parents continue to do this when the child is growing up two things can happen.

The first is that your child will rebel. As soon as a child feels that they can make their own decisions they will start to reject the ones you impose on them. This can be a tricky time for parents because they have to balance their child's growing ability to make choices against their concerns about their child's safety and security. Parents have to balance their own wishes against those of their child.

The second scenario is that your child will become a passive, uninvolved student who takes not responsibility or interest in learning. Parents who continually tell their children what to do and think deprive their child of the ability to be independent.

### Point out when people make an extra effort

Children may not understand the effort required to become proficient. Tell your child about the amount of training that goes into becoming a good dancer, the amount of work that goes into becoming a great athlete and the support that is behind every television star. Discuss how much effort things are going to take before you start a project. Then your child will gain some understanding of the effort he has to put into getting things finished.

Don't do this in a negative way. Do it in an encouraging way saying that all the work is worth the results.

# Attitudes about the future

Children need to feel <u>optimism</u> about what the future holds and be <u>able to handle change</u>

## Strategies that help children develop these skills

### Show your love

Children who feel loved are ready to take on the world. They know they have someone who will support then and help them be all that they are capable of being.

In a life that is busy and full of stress it can be difficult sometimes to take the time to show children that you love them. Children need constant reassurance; they need to know that you are on their side, and that you will love them no matter what they do. During your day take time to let your children know that you love them. You might say you love them, give them a hug, or express your love in other ways depending on the age of your child and the way your family expresses feelings.

Children who know they are loved have the confidence to face the future.

### Look forward to the future

Let your child hear you getting excited about future events. Too often parents pass on their doubts and concerns about what the future will bring. Children pick up on your comments and it affects how they think about the future

### Talk about upcoming events

When children know what is going to happen they feel less scared and more confident that they will be able to handle it.

### Embrace change

Welcome the changes that happen in your life and the life of your child. Be positive about the changes you notice and encourage your child to be positive about them too. Very young children can't wait to change, can't wait to grow up so they can do the things that their older siblings do. It can be very easy for parents to see these changes in a positive way. When your child gets older changes may go unnoticed or uncelebrated and that is a shame.

How important is it to notice changes in others and to comment on them?

Do you remember the last time you came home with a new haircut? Did your spouse notice? How would you have felt if the hadn't noticed, if they had said nothing?

Remember, change is good - and inevitable. Find ways of celebrating it.

### Change is a family affair

When one person in a family changes the rest of the family has to adapt and make changes themselves. It is very important that when you see your child changing and growing that you look at how you react to your child and change your behavior towards them.

## Plan and set goals

Plan to do something nice with your child – such as a trip to the zoo. Tell your child when this event will take place, maybe mark it on a calendar, and discuss how you will make this event happen.

Will you go with friends, take a bus, stay late? What will you see and do? Will you take photos and how will you do that? What will you do when you come home?

Questions like these help children prepare for the future event and make it feel more comfortable for them. They begin to feel that they can make plans for the future and set goals to get there.

## Remember the past then let it go

Children may have had frightening experiences in the past that stop them from going forward. For instance a child might have been frightened by a barking dog or by falling off play equipment. It is important to acknowledge your child's fears, explain why it won't happen again, and move on.

When children make mistakes at home or at school it is important that these mistakes are seen as learning experiences and the child is encouraged to try again.

## Happy talk

Children quickly pick up your feelings of frustration and worry. It is easy for parents to talk about the problems that are coming up in their lives. Parents worry about getting things done on time, about doing the shopping, seeing Aunty Jane, having enough money …

It is easy to pass on these fears to children and children may see them as being bigger than they really are. Try not to talk about your daily concerns with our child in ways that may make him fear for the future. Rather than saying, " It is going to be difficult to get the shopping done on time", say " I wonder what we can do to make shopping easier and quicker?".

Try and talk in a positive way about future activities so that you prevent your child becoming anxious.

## Ask "What if…?" questions

Make this into a game. As you are reading a book or walking down the street ask your child "What if the moon was made of cheese?" – and both of you come up with silly, or sensible, possibilities.

Take it in turns to ask a 'What if…" question and have fun with the answers!

## Ask your child what to do next

This is a fun game that helps children plan and feel that they have some control over future actions. Play this game when you are not in a hurry as you may be surprised by your child's answers and need to take time to work with them

Pretend that you don't know how to do something – such as setting the table for dinner or getting ready to go out. Ask your child for help. Can he tell you what you should do next?

Then try to do what your child tells you to do even if it means things go wrong.

For instance – your child might tell you to put your coat on before getting your shopping list. When something like this happens  - your child gets the order of actions wrong – do what your child suggests but point out the problem -  "How do I know what I need to buy?"

## Answer your child's questions

Children try to make sense of their world by asking questions, many questions, often at inappropriate moments. Always try to answer your child's questions or he will soon learn that asking questions does not get him answers and he will stop.

If you can't answer his question at the precise moment he asks it tell him when you will answer it – when you get home, after dinner etc. – and remember to make time to give him the answer!

## Do you remember when …?

A way of helping children understand the changes that have happened in their lives is to remind them of a previous time when they did something and to show them how much they have learned since that time.

"Do you remember when you couldn't catch a ball?"

"Now you can catch the ball you can play all kinds of games"

## I wonder how this works?

Children think that things work on their own, that there is some kind of magic mechanism that ensures things move and click and get onto store shelves.

Helping them understand how things work, that the engine makes the car move and the timer makes the alarm click and the milk in the carton comes from cows on the farm gives them a new way of understanding the things around them.

Better yet take them to a see a cow or give them an old watch to take to bits so that they understand what it takes to make things work.

## Go on adventures

Once a week, or once a month, tell your child that it is time to go on an adventure. Find something new to do with your child. Visit a museum or play park. Go to a different fast food restaurant. Go to school a different way. Get a book from the local library.

These adventures can be short or long but they help you and your child try out new experiences and discover new ways of doing things.

## Have fun with science

Get a book of simple science experiments from the library. Clear a space in the kitchen. Gather the equipment your child will need and let him try the experiments. Be ready to clear up the mess afterwards!

*Explore your natural surroundings.*

Help stimulate your child's curiosity by exploring what is in the natural world around him. Kids love bugs. Let your child discover the bugs and other wonders that live in your garden or the nearest park. Put a carrot top in a saucer of water and watch it grow. Let your child plant some bulbs in the garden or in a pot then in the spring he can enjoy the results.

*Help your child feel needed and important*

Children who feel needed and important are more likely to have the self-confidence to try new things and the optimism to try again when they fail. Help your child feel important by listening to what he says and commenting on his thoughts and by giving him simple tasks to do and telling him how much help he has been.

A child who feels that he has something to offer is more likely to accept change and move forward than one who feels insignificant.

# Cognitive Learning Skills

These are the skills your child needs in the classroom. These skills enable him or her to make sense of what is being taught and to produce work that reflects his or her abilities.

The cognitive skills are *attention*, *understanding*, *processing* and *production*.

# *Attention - the ability to selectively focus on specific information.*

## Strategies that develop the skill of attention

*Point*

Using words to direct your child's attention might not work. He has to think about what you have said and understand it before he starts to pay attention to it. A much quicker way to direct his or her attention is to point or touch what you want him to attend to. With young children who find it difficult to attend to something I use a pencil or a pointer to show exactly what they should be paying attention to.

*Eye contact*

When you want your child to pay attention to what you are saying it is important to ensure you have eye contact. When I am talking to a child and his attention is wandering I gently hold his head and look straight into his eyes. Then I can tell when his attention is wandering and I can help him refocus.

*Look at me when I am talking!*

Normally we expect people to look at us when we are talking to them. Children may find this difficult to do and it is easy for them to become distracted and not listen to what you are saying.

There are five things you can do to prevent this.

1.  Gently move your child until she is looking at you
2.  Move into a position where you are in front of your child and she has to look at you.  This can be particularly effective when you stand between your child and the screen he is watching!
3.  Don't say anything to your child until she is in a position to give you her full attention
4.  Never talk to your child while you are walking away from him
5.  Never listen to your child if he is talking to you while walking away

### *Look at your child when she is talking!*

Be a role model. When your child has something to say to you make sure that you pay attention to her!

### *Ask the right question\ask for more information*

Ask your child the type of questions that help him direct his attention.
Here is a list of questions to use.

*   What is…?

*   Where is…?

*   Why did…?

*   When did…?

*   Which one…?

*   When did … happen?

*   Who was…?

*   Can you tell me three things about…?

### *Make sure your child is aware of the issue*

No child is going to pay attention to something that has no meaning for him.  What might have meaning for you may not have meaning for your child. You need to make sure that your child understands why he has to pay attention to something.

Here are some questions that will help your child be more aware of the issue.

*   What do you think we have to do here?

*   What can we do?

*   What do you think will happen if…?

*   Can you see a problem here?

- What do we need?

### Make it their problem!

There is nothing that gets children's attention more than having to sort out their own problems! It may seem quicker to solve your child's problems for them rather than waiting for them to stumble through their ideas. But if you always do this your child will not learn how to solve his own problems.

If you want your child to pay attention to something – make it their problem! For example - If you want your child to pick up their clothes – don't wash any clothes you find on the floor. If you want your child to finish a task don't give him TV time until it is finished.

### Ask your child to repeat what you have said

When your child learns that there may be going to be a test she is more likely to pay attention to what you say. By doing this you are also checking that your child has understood what you have said.

### Simplify how you talk to your child.

Have you ever seen anyone's eye's go glassy when there are just too many words to listen to? Don't let this happen to your child.

Keep your sentences short and use simple words whenever you can. You might have to limit the number of things you give your child to do at one time. It is easier for a child to pay attention to " Take your shoes upstairs" that to " Pick up your shoes, make sure they are clean, find your socks and take them all upstairs'.

### Use a special sign

Let your child know that when you really need him to pay attention you will give him a special sign. This could be raising your hand, clapping your hands, whatever works for you and your child. Many teachers get the attention of their class by holding up one hand. The children have learned this sign means they have to listen.

### Allow time

Give your child time to pay attention to something before asking her to act on it.

For instance, it is better to say, "Look at that store window – (pause) – what do you want to buy?" than "What do you want to buy from the store?"

### Pay attention to the signals you give

You may be asking your child to pay attention to you while you are distracted.

If you want your child to pay attention to you, you must pay attention to him.

### Schedule breaks.

Paying attention to something takes energy. When your child needs to pay attention for long times make sure that you schedule breaks. This applies to watching TV or video games as well as learning something new.

## Games that improve attention

There are some simple games you can play with your child that help develop this skill.

### Missing word games
Leave a word out of a story or rhyme and see if your child notices it.

### Play 'Simon Says'
The child has to listen carefully to win the game.

### Memory games
These are great to play in the car. Start a sentence such as " I went to the store and I bought cake". Your child then adds onto that sentence – " I went to the store and I bought Cake and ice cream". See how long you can make the list before someone gets it wrong!

### What can you see that is…?
This is also a good game to play in the car. It encourages children to look carefully. Ask questions such as, 'What can you see that is blue?', 'What can you see that moves?' or 'What can you see that is round?'

### Looking games
Books such as 'Where's Waldo' can help your child pay attention to the picture on the page or you can ask your child to look at a picture in a book for a few seconds then close the book and see what she can remember. You can make this into a game by seeing who can remember the most number of things in the picture.

### Puzzles
Jigsaw puzzles help children look carefully to find missing pieces. They help children pay attention to important aspects of each piece.

Computer games are good too. Children have to pay attention if they are going to solve them. Once you know that your child can attend to a puzzle long enough to solve it you know that he can attend to you or his teacher for the same amount of time.

## Use your child's name
Everyone is conditioned to react when they hear their name. If you want to get your child's attention start by saying their name then follow through with instructions. For example, "Sarah, I need your help!" is better than, "I need your help!"

## Always read the instructions
A reason older students have difficulty paying attention to their work is because they

have not taken time to read the instructions. When a student knows what he or she is expected to do it is easy for them to direct their attention to the task. Always check that your child has read the instructions before work starts.

# Understanding - developing the ability to use language and space

## Strategies to develop the skill of understanding

### Put words to what you see and hear

Children need a good vocabulary if they are to understand what they hear and see. You can help them develop a good vocabulary by putting words to what you see and hear. Rather than tell your child that his sweater is in his bedroom, tell him that it is IN the closet, BESIDE the bed, ON a hook. This way you are developing your child's spatial vocabulary and understanding.

The more words you use the more your child will learn. Some parents limit the way they talk to their children, believing that some sort of baby talk will help their child understand more easily. Baby talk is fine for a short time but even very young children can understand long words. Children need to learn as many words as possible so that the can learn their meaning and use them to further their thinking. The more words you use to describe what you see, hear and do, the larger your child's vocabulary will become.

### Self talk

I love telling parents about this way of helping develop their child's understanding. It is so easy to do, requires no special resources and can be fun.

This process works because your child is a curious being and will be intrigued by what you are doing and saying. You can use this process whenever your child is within hearing range yet you do not have to tell your child to do anything; it is you doing the work. All you have to do is talk. Talk about what you are doing, why you are doing it, what you will do next, what you are concerned about, why you hate the dog…, talk about anything and everything. Your child will be listening. Not only will he be listening he will be learning new words, new ideas, and new strategies.

If there is something special you want your child to learn about or do then you can structure your 'self talk' to address that issue.

I know that some parents find it strange to use 'self talk'. We have all been told that talking to oneself is pointless and very few of us have any experience of ding this. I recommend you practice by talking to your reflection in a mirror until you feel happy about using self-talk.

### Say what you mean

This can be hard to do. We rarely use language that is precise and clear. It is no wonder that children have difficulty understanding what we tell them. Think about how you talk to your child and try to make what you say as clear and unambiguous as possible.

### Don't be afraid of using long words

The more words you use the more words your child will learn. Some parents limit the way they talk to their children believing that some sort of baby talk will help their child understand more easily. Use simple clear sentences but don't avoid long words when they make sense.

### Be an active listener

Do not interrupt your child when he is talking to you. Listen carefully and when he has finished you can restate what he has said using different – and better words. That way your child will know that what he has said was understood and also that there is a better way of saying it.

### Expand sentences

You don't have to go overboard with this but when you change "Look at that dog!" to, "Look at that brown dog with the red collar!" you are helping your child develop his vocabulary and pay attention to detail.

### Play word games

Any word games! They all help your child understand language.

### Go beyond 'housekeeping' words

You know the kids of words I mean – the ones you use everyday to get things done, the ones you never even think about, "Do this", "Get that", "Come here" – housekeeping talk!

Children develop better language skills when parents go beyond housekeeping talk. When you ask your child to do something give reasons. Here are three examples of how to do that.

"Please get that so we can take it with us when we leave."

" Do your homework so that you can watch TV later".

"Come here and we will read a book together".

### Don't fill in missing words

You know your child well and you can often guess what your child trying to say. You 'fill in the gaps' for your child. Doing this will not help him or her develop language skills. When talking with your child give her time to find the words she needs and resist all temptation to help her by assuming what she is going to say.

### Say and Draw Game

This is a game where one person describes a simple diagram or picture that they are looking at and the other person has to reproduce it by listening to what the person says. It is not as easy as it seems. This is a good way to help your child be very specific about the words he uses.

### Ask HOW questions

Surprisingly, people hardly ever ask this kind of question. It can be used to help children understand how they are thinking as well as improving their understanding. Some 'How' questions to use …

- How did you do that?

- Yes, that's right but how do you know it's right?

- How is this one better than the other?

- How did you know how to do that?

### Check the little words

It is the little words that are crucial to understanding. Words such as on, under, beside, on top of, around, few, smaller, between, before, later by, etc. Make sure your child understand them all!

### Check, check, check

You ask your child to do something and you expect him to be able to do it. You know the words that came out of your mouth were clear and precise.  But do you know what your child heard or what words he listened to? There can be big differences between what you say and what your child hears. Never assume that your child has understood what you have said to him.

Use this three-step process to ensure your child has understood you.

First, get your child's attention and tell her what you her to do. Then ask her to repeat what you said. Lastly, I ask him if he has any questions about what you told her.

Only then can you be sure your child has understood. Check, check, check, that you child understands and avoid mistakes of miscommunication and all the trouble they lead to.

### The army way

My father taught me this. He said that in the army you were told the same thing three ways to make sure that you understood what to do. I think it is great way of helping children (and others) understand what you are telling them. It goes like this - Tell your child what you are going to tell him. Tell him and then tell him what you just told him.

Here is an example –

Jonny, we need to talk about visiting Grandma. We are going in a couple of weeks and staying for the weekend. Now you know when we are going do you have anything to say?

### Know what interests your child

… and talk about it! This is a good way to increase language skills and understanding.

### Let children play

Children learn language quickly when they use it in play. Games of imagination are particularly useful for learning new words.

### I am thinking of …

You gradually describe an object that you are thinking about. After each description give your child a chance to guess what it is. For example – I am thinking of something that is in the house… It is square… It has four legs … It is made of wood ….

### Schedule 'Talking Time'

Set a side a few minutes every day as talking time, when you and your child can spend time together to talk about anything that interests either of you.

### Alike and different

Choose two objects – see who can come up with the most number of ways they are alike and different. For example, a table and carpet are alike because they are in houses, on the floor, and they both get dirty. They are different because one is hard, one is soft, you stand on one and sit on the other, and one is made of wood the other of wool. See who can come up with the most examples.

### Silly Why?

In this word game you and your child try to come up with silly reasons for things. An example, "Why do you wear shoes?" "So that the sidewalk can't bite my toes!"

### Direction game

Stand still and ask your child to get you into another room. Do exactly what your child tells you to do. See how carefully your child can use words to give you clear directions. Take care not to bump into furniture!

### Read instructions

If all else fails, read the instructions! We often try to do things without taking the time to understand how to do it. Don't let your child fall into this habit. Show her how important instructions are and how helpful they can be,

### The language of Math

Children often struggle to understand math problem because of the specialized language used. Words such as denominator or factor can cause a child panic if not properly understood. The language of math needs to be taught very carefully and if you or your child is unsure about the meaning of a word ask the teacher for an explanation.

# Processing

The ability to process information requires a child to *relate new learning to old* and to have *a plan of action.*

## Strategies to help your child develop skills of processing

### Make a plan

Let your child see you making plans and how to make them work. Let him see how one action leads to another and that without thinking of how this happens the plan will fail.

For instance – make a plan for getting ready for school or an outing. Talk about the first thing you have to do, then the next, and so on until the plan is complete. Talk about what would happen if you missed out one of the steps in the plan. Would the plan still work?

### Help your child make a plan

This is a way of building relationships between things, each step of a plan has to relate to the one before it, and the one after it, or the plan will not work.

Sometimes children cannot see flaws in the plans they make. When a child has not 'thought things through' the plan will not work. Rather than getting annoyed or exasperated with your child you might need to help him or her think about the missing steps. He or she may not understand the relationship between situations.

### Play 'What if…?'

This is a relationship building game, a way to try out relationships in a safe way. By asking "What if…?" you are asking your child to think about how one thing may be connected to another.

Here are a few questions to start with. I am sure that you can think of many others.

- What if the moon was made of cheese?

- What if you didn't finish your homework?

- What if we went out for ice cream?

- What if the house turned upside down?

These questions raise awareness of cause and effect relationships in fun and meaningful ways. Children have wonderful imaginations and should be able to think of fantastic answers to these questions.

### Have fun learning

Children remember and learn best when they are having fun! Make learning fun. Use games, books, toys, that you and your child enjoy. If you and your child are doing something that is not fun – STOP.

## Play

Children learn through play. Play is a child's job. Make sure that your child has chance to play every day – both on her own and with others.

## Self talk – cause/effect

Self-talk (purposefully talking to yourself within your child's hearing) is a good way to help children understand the relationship between cause and effect. Talk about something you did, and what happened as a result. Talk about how you would change something you did in order to get a better outcome.

Your child will come to understand the process of cause and effect in new ways.

## Limit stress

Brains cannot work when they are stressed. Do not expect your child to be able to think if he is under any kind of stress. Do whatever you can to understand why and when your child is under stress and do something to fix it before you try to help him learn.

## Watch your language!

Whatever you say to your child either helps or hinders their thinking. Think about that statement for a minute, it is a powerful statement to make but I believe it to be true. Whatever you say to your child either helps them develop their processing skills or stops them from developing these skills.

There are two ways you can talk to your child.

When you talk to a child in a way that stops them thinking, that closes down their need to think, it is called using *closed language*. Statements such as, 'Do this', 'Put that there', 'Eat your dinner', are all closed. Your child has no reason to think about what to do or why he has to do it.  His thinking is closed, shut down.

If you talk to your child in a way that stimulates your child's thinking it is called using *open language*. Often open language is a question that makes the child think.  Why did you do that?  How can we finish this? Where shall we put this?  Your child has to think of an answer, he has to process information and come up with a solution.

Be aware that how you talk with your child influences how well your child thinks.

## Do you remember when/who?

This can be a great way of helping your child solve present problems by relating them to past experiences.

- Do you remember when you did this before? What did you do?

- Do you remember when you gave away that toy?  How did it make you feel?

- Do you remember when you saw that word before? What did it say?

### Twenty questions

Children love this game and soon develop strategies that help them get the answer quickly. Someone thinks of something – anything. The other person can ask 20 questions to try to find out what it is. The first person has to answer honestly.

(Hint – some basic questions such as 'Is it inside or outside?' and "Can I see it now?' are a good way to get started!)

### Mad minutes

Use a timer. How many girls' names can you say in a minute? How many animals? How many things you eat?

This game develops memory, understanding of relationships, awareness of categories, and it is good fun!

### Sleep on it

Brains are wonderful things. They often sort out problems by themselves. If your child has trouble working something out tell him to sleep so that his brain can work – true!

### 'Exploding keys'

Memory is an important part of understanding. One way to remember something is to link what has to remember to some big emotional issue. When I put my keys down I imagine a big explosion ad the damage it would do to the surroundings. It really helps me remember where my keys are when I need them.

### Pictures in your head

Children who are Picture Smart may not be good at using words to help them think. If your child has difficulty putting thinking into words ask him or her to tell you about the 'pictures in their head' as a way of understanding what he is thinking about.

# Production

The ability to produce good work requires skills of **effort and accuracy** as well as an understanding of what the *finished work should look like*.

## Strategies that help your child develop skills of production

### What 'finished' looks like

How can we expect a child to know what his work should look like unless we show him? Children may have no idea how things should end up looking. When you do a jigsaw puzzle you use the picture to help you know where to put the pieces. If you did not know what you were aiming for it would be incredibly difficult to finish the puzzle.

Children need to understand what they are aiming for, what the finished product (a tidy room, a good book report?) looks like and feels like. Only then, after your child knows what to achieve can you start to help her achieve it.

If you want your child to put all the toys away show your child how good the room looks when he does this.

If you want your child to read a book show him how many pages or chapters it has.

If you want your child to complete a work page show him what a finished work page looks like.

### How to get to 'finished'

Your child may know what she wants to achieve but may not know how to achieve it. Help her make a plan so that she understands all the steps she has to take to get to her goal. You can talk through this plan with your child or write it down and cross off each step as it is completed The plan will help your child understand the amount of effort she will need to finish the task.

### Praise the process not the product

We want children to produce good work, to finish things and to do them well and it is important to say how good the finished product looks. But it is more important to praise your child for all the effort he has put into getting his work finished. By praising the process rather than the product you are encouraging your child to repeat the actions that led to success.

### Take your time

Make sure your child has enough time to finish what she is doing. It is difficult for children to assess how long it will take to get things done. If your child wants to do something that will take some time help her break the process into several small so she understands how long it will take to complete the task.

### Ask 'So what?'

Children like to finish their work quickly and then go onto the next thing they have to do. This means they miss the big picture. They may not link what they have done to what they have learned. When your child has completed something encourage him to take a few minutes to review his work, to step back from it and to see it as part of a bigger process.

That way they have a better chance of remembering what they did and how they did it and are more ready to do the same next time.

Example –

After reading a book (or a page in a book) take time to talk about the story, the part your child liked best, the pictures he saw and how hard or easy it was for him to understand.

Use these questions to help your child think about what he has done.

- So what did you learn?

- So what does it mean?

- So what do you think about this?

- So what do you do next?

- So what use will this be?

- So what does it feel like?

- So what will happen now?

- So what did you do?

- So what do you suppose...?

These questions will help your child summarize their learning and make it part of their knowledge bank.

### You do, I do

This is a way to help children complete tasks that they think are too big or difficult for them to do. Rather than trying to make your child do something that he does not want to do use this process to share the task.

Set limits. Decide how much each of you will do before it is the other person's turn. (Put away one toy?  Do one sum?  Carry one shopping bag?)

Decide who is going to start – you or your child.

You do – the person who has been chosen to start does the first part of the task.

I do – then the other person does the next part of the task.

 Repeat until the task is finished!

Give yourselves lots of praise for finishing the task and for helping each other.

### Practice makes perfect

Children underestimate the amount of practice it takes to do things well. They see you doing things well and assume that they can do it as well as you. They may not know how many times you have done this before or how many times you got it wrong before you learned how to do it well. When they fail to get something right the first time they can get very disappointed and think that they can't do it at all.

Make sure that you tell your child how you had to practice to be able to do things well. And share all the mistakes you made, it will make your child feel much better and he will be ready to try again when he fails.

### Let your child fail

This may seem harsh but it is only by failing that children learn. Don't jump in and try to help when you see your child making a mistake. Stand back and be ready to help only if and when he asks for help.

Children need to learn to do things for themselves. If you do everything for your child he will become passive and dependent and afraid to try anything new.

### Give praise - but within boundaries

Children know when they have done something well and they know when they could have done better. Praising children for doing something that they could have done better lets them think that they do not have to try as hard next time! It makes them lazy.

When your child does sloppy work say something like, " Well I see that you have finished but I am not sure you did it as well as you could. What do you think?"

In my experience children are relieved when they know that you know they could do better. Don't make a big deal of it.  Don't make your child redo the task. But do let your child know that you expect more from him next time.

### Measure progress

Checklists work wonders! Children love crossing off things that they have completed. There are different types of checklists. Choose which one works for you and your child.

1.  A checklist of the steps for completing a single task

2.  A checklist of all the tasks to be completed that day

3.  A of whenever your child does something good  (this is like a star chart)

4.  A checklist of all the jobs you have to do  (so that your child can see that you have to go through the same process)

Make up your own kind of checklist. Make it look pretty and fun to complete and put it somewhere you can both see it.

### Limit distractions

Find a quiet space to do things, turn off the TV, and put the dog in another room. Give your child a chance to focus on the task at hand. Young children are more easily distracted than older children so do not expect a very young child to concentrate on one task for too long. But, be prepared to be surprised!  When children are interested in what they are doing they can concentrate for much longer than you think!

### Get rid of clutter

Some children work well surrounded by clutter but most children find it distracting. Clear a space to get a job done. Line up all the things your child will need (pencil, paper, scissors etc.) before he starts a task. That way he will not have to stop and interrupt what he is doing to get what he needs.

### What motivates your child?

Most parents know what motivates their child because they have had years of trying to get him or her to do things. But you need to be aware of two issues.

1.  Children's motivation changes

2.   What motivates your child might be very different from what motivates you

And remember, intrinsic motivation beats extrinsic motivation every time! Rather than give your child a reward for doing something (extrinsic) tell him how proud he has made you feel.

### Slice and dice

Some tasks can look daunting to a child, far too big for him or her to handle. So rather than try and fail they find reasons for not doing the task at all. This is when you need to 'slice and dice'.

Take that big task and break it down into a series of small tasks that don't look so difficult. Then tell your child how doing all the small tasks helped him get the big task finished!

### Look for alternatives

There are many ways to get something done. If one way doesn't work try another. Ask your child if he can think of a better way to get something done. You might be surprised by his answer!

### Have a big WHY

Children need to know why they are being asked to do something. The bigger the WHY the more they understand and want to get the job done. Make the WHY about them as much as possible.

For example, if you ask your child to pick up his clothes and the only reason you can think of is because you want him to – that is not a big enough 'why'. If you ask him because you tell him it will leave room for him to play his favorite game that might be the 'why' he needs.

### Celebrate success!

This is the final, important, link in the whole learning process. Celebrate success either by praising your child for a job well done, sharing a cookie, going for a walk – whatever you both want to do. The 'feel good' effect of doing this sets your child up for the next task!

# Strategies for 'Make School Make Sense'

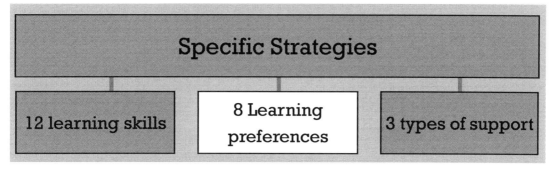

Children struggle to learn when the way they are taught does not match the way they learn. Children learn in different ways. According to Gardner there are eight main ways children like to learn. Everyone learns using a unique mix of these eight ways.

## 8 Learning Preferences

| | |
|---|---|
| *People Smart* | *Picture Smart* |
| *Self Smart* | *Nature Smart* |
| *Word Smart* | *Music Smart* |
| *Number Smart* | *Body Smart* |

- Self Smart learners learn best when they can work things out for themselves

- People Smart learners prefer to try ideas out on others

- Word Smart learners learn by talking, reading, writing and listening

- Number Smart learners like a logical structure to their learning

- Body Smart learners learn best when they are moving

- Nature Smart learners prefer to be connected to the natural world

- Music Smart learners learn using rhythm and rhyme

- Picture Smart learners like diagrams and visual images to help them learn

Teachers rarely teach in ways that facilitate all eight ways of learning. Teachers expect students to learn by listening, reading, writing and speaking and lessons tend to have set structures and patterns. This is a style of teaching that appeals to students who are mainly Word Smart or Number Smart.

Classes may allow students to interact with each other, providing People Smart learners with a situation that suits them but most classes expect students to learn while at their desk, a learning context that works well for students who are mainly Self Smart.

Picture Smart learners are well served to about 8 years of age then the teaching changes to a much more word focused approach that some find confusing. This change in teaching style is why many students who were doing well in Grade 3 begin to struggle in Grade 4.

Students who are mainly Nature Smart or Music Smart may find that there is very little teaching that focuses on how they like to learn and students who are Body Smart may struggle to learn in a classroom that has limits on how much students can move around.

The free diagnostic learning assessment at www.Vnaya.com will help you understand your child's unique learning preferences and the strategies that follow will help you provide your child with learning opportunities that match these preferences.

Using the results from the Porter Diagnostic Learning Assessment look at the section that relates to your child's preferred way of learning and choose one or more strategies to use with your child. If your child has more than one learning preference look at all the sections that relate to how your child likes to learn.

Each section describes how a particular type of learner learns best and then gives you strategies to use to help your child benefit from schooling, homework help and tutoring. There are phrases you can use with your child while encouraging them to do homework.

# People Smart

## Description

Children who are People Smart are able to pick up on the mood, characteristics, emotions, and intentions of those around them. They are able to use this information when they interact with others.

People Smart students enjoy being around others and work well with them. They know what is going on with everybody around them and quickly pick up on other people's feelings and intentions. They are natural leaders among peers and groups and easily form strong, positive relationships with others.

They have an open personality, are eager to please and are often very good at helping resolve conflicts between peers. They can be skilled verbal and nonverbal communicators and are able to influence the opinions and actions of others

People with a highly developed People Smarts can get along with almost everyone they meet, and are almost never shy.

However, this type of learner can be stubborn and inflexible and may read too much into someone's actions and feel affronted as a result. Some People Smart Learners have problems dealing with authority and may use their skills to start conflicts rather than to solve them. People Smart students do not learn well when they have to rely on their own skills without access to help from others.

## People Smart Learners and schooling

### Type of school

Whether or not a People Smart learner is allowed to use his skills in the classroom depends on the type of school and the philosophy of the teacher. A People Smart student will not learn well if the school discourages collaborative work and expects students to work on their own.

These are the children who long for recess to arrive so they can talk with their friends, who are often in trouble for chatting in class, who volunteer to look after the new student, and who can anticipate what the teacher will do next.

If they like the teacher there is nothing they will not do for them, but if there is a personality clash they may be disruptive in class.

They need a classroom situation where they can work with others, mix and mingle, exchange ideas, try out their ideas and revise them before handing them in.

If your child attends a school that encourages collaborative learning all is well. If your child attends a school that has a traditional approach to teaching and learning - children sit at desks all day with few opportunities for interaction with other students - you need create a more cooperative learning situation at home.

## Strategies for helping People Smart Learners in school

### Discuss learning preferences

Explain to your child that some children learn best when they work by themselves and that many classrooms are set up for this type of learner. Explain that interacting with others at this time will be seen as a problem and that he or she might get into trouble.

### Social times

Talk to your child about the times he or she can socialize in school. People Smart learners may get into trouble for talking and need to know when it is OK to do so.

### Alone time

These students may not realize that they may be expected to work on their own for large parts of the school day. Help your child understand this by explaining why and when he or she needs to spend time working by him or herself.

### Talk to the teacher

Let the teacher know that your child is People Smart and likes to work and learn with others. Get to know when group projects will happen in class so that you can tell your child and keep him or her motivated through the times when solitary work is required.

### Silent reading

Many classrooms need students to spend time reading and some insist that this is 'silent' time. A People Smart learner will find it difficult to concentrate, as he or she will want to talk about what is being read. You can help your child improve his or her reading skills and reading comprehension by having a copy of the book at home and reading it with your child. You can use this time to ask questions, make comments and discuss the book – all ways to help your People Smart learner interact with you and the words on the page.

### Trouble in class

It is not unusual for this type of learner to try to interact with other students during work times. This can lead to talking at inappropriate moments or even to bothering other students. This behavior may not be acceptable and you may need to explain to your child that other children prefer to work on their own.

### Not self starters

People Smart learners like to be told what to do and how to do it. They may be unwilling to start work when they are unsure about what the teacher wants. This type of learner needs good clear directions.

## Strategies to help with homework

### Kitchen table

This type of learner likes to be with people, to share and discuss ideas and thoughts. They work best when there are people around and prefer to work at the kitchen table rather than in their room.

### Social media limits

These students may use technologies such as Internet, social media such as 'facebook' and other ways of being part of a group. This helps them feel connected with others and to exchange ideas and insights. Of course, the downside is that these children can spend so much time connecting with others that the never get any work done. Set limits on the amount of time your child can do this.

### Talking time

Be ready to talk to your child about their homework and discuss ways that you can help. Share your ideas about their work and listen to their ideas. This type of learner likes to talk over problems with others before settling on a solution. They use this collaborative time to help them think.

## Give advice

This type of learner appreciates being given advice but that does not mean he or she will act on it. Do not be surprised if after you have given your child advice he or she ignores it and does things differently.

## Time to socialize.

People Smart learners need to socialize. When doing homework they need frequent breaks so they can talk to you or their friends. Set a time limit for this interaction so it does not distract from their work.

## Chat first

Take time to chat with your child about the work they have to do. Discuss what work they will do first, what will be easy to do, and plan how they will get the work done. Talking through these issues before they start will help them be organized and focused.

## Teaching others

This type of learner likes to share what they can do. Ask your child to show you how they did their work. Children remember more of what they have learned if they can each it to others. Encourage your child to help younger siblings with their work.

## Using the words 'us' and 'we'

People Smart children like to be included in activities, so always talk about 'us' or 'we' to help them feel part of a group.

## Family recognition

Use checklists or schedules so that your child can show you what work he is doing and when it gets finished. A People Smart learner needs others to know what he is doing.

## You then me

These learners like to share. If your young child is struggling or needs motivation suggest that you do one math question, or read one sentence, and he does the next.

## Good clear directions

Before your child starts homework make sure that he or she knows exactly what they have to do. Check they have understood the directions and know how to do their work.

## Discussions

Learning from books is a lonely process but one that a child needs to be able to do. When your child has book learning to do help him retain the information by asking him to talk to you about it and by starting a discussion of some of the main points.

## Post-it notes

These act as 'conversation' pieces for your child. Keep a supply handy and get him to note down the main ideas from his work - or even his thoughts and complaints!

### Email/text messages

This is a good way to keep in touch with others who are at a distance.

### Homework club

Students can help each other - just make sure the other learners are People Smart too!

### Collaborative projects

Sharing the workload with others and working together to create one project is a great way to motivate these learners.

## Words that help when you are helping with homework

Choose one or more of these phrases and use them when you are helping your child with homework.

'Let's work on this together'
'We can work this out'
'Tell me what you are thinking'
'Help me understand this'
'Let's discuss this'
'Let's explore our options'

## People Smart Learners and tutoring

### Type of tutor

These learners learn best when there is social interaction. It is important to find a tutor who understands your child's need to talk, to try out ideas, and to be given feedback about their work.

Your child needs a tutor who will be their friend as well as their teacher. When the personality of the tutor matches that of your child all will be well. If there is a clash of personalities, if your child does not get on well with the tutor, then you need to find another tutor.

### Type of program

Tutoring programs where your child is learning with others will work for this type of learner. Make sure that your child has chance to interact with other learners before you decide to put your child in a tutoring program. Some programs have several children in a group but do not allow for much interaction.

*Involve your child in the process*

Involve your child in the process of getting a tutor. Explain why he needs a tutor, what he will learn, and how you are going to find a tutor. Also, tell your child that, if he is not happy with the tutor (not the need for tutoring) after three sessions you will talk with him about the possibility of getting a different tutor.

# Self-Smart

## Description

Students who are Self Smart learners are skilled at self-reflection and know themselves very well. They are in touch with themselves, who they are, what they need, and what they can accomplish. They have the ability to understand themselves, appreciate their own feelings, fears and motivations. They sense their own strengths and weaknesses and follow their own instincts rather than the crowd. When they are not sure of their feelings they can become restless and unsettled.

Self-Smart learners know their own minds and like to work things out for themselves before sharing their ideas. This often makes them poor at communicating because they assume that everyone thinks the same way they do. They are self-motivated and use their feelings to guide their behavior. They like to spend time alone and can be uncomfortable in crowds.

## Self Smart Learners and schooling

*Type of school*

The Self-Smart learner prefers a school that has a traditional approach to teaching, where students are expected to work on their own. This type of learner is happy to sit at a desk and do work without interacting with others.

Self Smart learners do well in most schools where children are expected to learn on their own, to get on with their work. These children may secretly enjoy taking test or exams because they are expected to work on their own without help from others.

They like individual project work where they can express their ideas, but may struggle to contribute to group work, complaining that the other students will not listen to them.

Teachers like Self Smart students. They can be relied on to get on with their work and only ask for help after they have tried and failed to solve their problems. But sometimes these students will have high expectations that are too difficult to reach and will think that they must use their own skills to solve l their problems rather than seeking the help they need. When this happens they can become frustrated and angry with themselves.

*Strategies that help*

There is not much you need to do to help a Self Smart learner in school. However you need to be aware when this type of learner is struggling to learn and needs help. He or she may not ask for help until it is too late and they become frustrated about their seeming lack of ability to learn. You need to watch for signs of frustration and avoidance and try to discover why this is happening.

Also do not get frustrated when you know your Self Smart learner could do better. This type of learner is not good at showing people how bright he or she is. That does not mean thy do not need recognition for their work and successes. This type of learner assumes you know how bright he or she is and expects you to acknowledge that. Lack of praise can lead them to become depressed.

## Self Smart Learners and homework

### Own space
These students like to do homework in a space that is theirs and where they will not get disturbed. Unlike People Smart learners who work best with others around this learner would prefer to work in his or her room.

### Trust
This learner expects to be trusted to get his or her work done. If you are constantly checking that work is finished he or she may become angry and stressed. Set the 'rules' and expectations about homework first then send them off and assume the work will get done. You might set a time to check the work if you think this is necessary.

### Self-Assessment
These students know what they know, they know themselves and what they have learned. If you ask nicely they will tell you, but on their own terms. Do not expect them to tell you what homework assignments they have to do. That is why you have to set the rules beforehand so that everyone understands expectations.

### Self-determination
They also feel that they are quite capable of making their own decisions about where they want to go and what they want to do in life. After all, they have been thinking about this for some time so of course they have it all worked out! This makes them very difficult to help. Talk to your child and negotiate how and when he or she will ask you for help. Tell your child that you will not interfere unless asked.

### Quiet time
Quiet time, doing something they want to do, helps them get back in touch with the world. However, time alone may not be quiet time. Your child may be processing so many thoughts and feelings that he or she never gets time to relax. Set time limits for homework and allow your child to relax by doing something he or she loves.

## Daydreaming

Daydreaming is how this type of learner gets in touch with is or her thoughts. Do not assume that when your child is daydreaming they are not thinking. However, if the teacher tells you that your child daydreams in class you should explain to him or her that there are good times and bad times to do this and that the first ten minutes of any lesson are crucial and your child must pay attention.

## Private conversations

Not for them the large discussion group, unless they can tell everyone what they think. You will get more out of this child (or into him) with quiet chats where no one else is listening. Don't talk about homework with others around the table. Find a time when you can be alone with your child before you bring up the subject.

## 'I' activities

Group activities can be hard for this type of learner. When your child takes a break from homework he or she needs to do something by his or herself, maybe even go for a solitary walk. You need to allow your child 'I' activities – 'I would like to….', 'I will …'.

## Problem solving

This type of learner does so much 'in-their-head' thinking that problem solving comes naturally to them. Allow your child time to come up with solutions to problems. When your child goes quiet and reflective it is because he or she is working out what to do. They might not share their solutions with you but they are thinking all the time.

Watch out when they can't work something out though! Your child will get frustrated and angry and you need to be ready to jump in and help.

## Ask about feelings

Helping your child understand his or her feelings about their work will help them, and you, find ways to make the work more palatable. If your child tells you he hates math you can ask him why. He may say it is too difficult or too boring or that he hates his teacher. Whatever his reason you can be ready with a reply.

## Self help books

Self-Learners like to discover more about how they can improve their knowledge and thinking. These students use Google, Wikipedia and the library with ease. Make sure they have easy access to these programs.

## Success lists

Because this type of learner finds it very hard to recognize their achievements they can easily lose self-confidence and may even become depressed. Writing a daily list of successes helps to boost their self-confidence.

## Make a plan

These learners need a sense of direction and a plan on how to get there. If you ask your child if he has a plan for getting his work done he will probably tell you that he has. These learners can be very good at making plans for themselves.   However, if they are not sure how to do something and, as a result, cannot make a plan they procrastinate and delay doing their work. If you see this happening you need to step in and help them plan their next move.

### *Avoid repetition*

This type of learner hates to repeat what he already knows. Homework that is set to practice a particular skill can be boring for them. They will need some extra motivation to complete this type of work.

### *Setting goals*

Goals help this type of learner to focus on what has to be done. These goals should be personal for instance rather than having a goal to finish work the goal could be to finish it before a certain time or before you have made dinner.

### *Time to reflect*

These children are good thinkers. They prefer to think things through before starting on a task. Remind your child to take a few minutes to reflect on their work before they start.

### *Self-evaluation*

Ask your child how well she did her work. For this type of learner self-evaluation is as important as teacher evaluation. If she feels she has done good work chances are the teacher will too.

### *Independent study*

Self Smart learners like to be given a topic and then be set free to explore it in their own way. Don't tell you child what to do or how to do it unless you receive a request for help.

### *Words to use when helping with homework*

'Do you know how to do this?
'You can work this out'
'May I tell you what I think?'
'Tell me what you are thinking'
'Let me know if you need help
'Have you explored your options?'

## Self Smart Learners and tutoring

### *Type of tutor*

These students do not need to be 'friends' with a tutor. They would rather have a tutor they respected than one who tried to be friendly and easy going. Your child will work best with a tutor who is a subject specialist rather than a generalist who can help your child set learning goals and a plan on how to get there.

Try to find a tutor who is Self Smart. A People Smart tutor may try to interfere in your child's thinking process and your child would find this annoying.

This type of learner expects the tutor to understand how they think and may not be good at explaining their thinking to a tutor. The tutor needs to refrain from questioning them too closely as this type of learner may feel that this questioning is a sign that the tutor does not trust them to think things through.

### *Type of program*

Self-Smart learners prefer one-to-one tutoring rather than being in a group. This can be expensive so to be sure that you get the best tutor and value for money read the section on Extra support.

# Word Smart

## Description

Children who are **Word Smart** use words to help them learn. What do we mean by 'words'? If you think about it, words can be spoken, read and written. So a Word Smart child will learn best by talking, reading and writing. Children who are Word Smart tend to have a very good vocabulary and know the meaning of many words. They use language well, understand jokes, are good storytellers and can express their thoughts verbally and in writing. For them, reading is a great way of learning.

Word Smart learners think in words. They may be good spellers because they like words and take notice of them. Their skills are useful in all aspect of life, from reading road signs to classic novels, from writing emails to composing poetry, from telling a child what they want them to do to discussing politics.

Parents often ask me about the best way to help their young child succeed in school. I tell them that the best help they can give their child is to talk to them, to help their children understand language and how it can be used. I can teach any child who can talk to me and express thoughts and feelings. It is those children who do not know how to communicate, who remain closed books that I find difficult to know how to help.

## Word Smart Learners and schooling

### Type of school

Almost any type of school will work for a child who is Word Smart. Most teaching is word based and nearly all standardized tests emphasize this way of being smart.

However it is easy to take being Word Smart for granted and to assume the child has understood what is taught. Everyone uses words to talk, write or read so everyone is Word Smart to some degree. There are different levels and ways of being Word Smart. A shop worker does not need to use the same level of language as a professor, a young child does not need the vocabulary of an adult and an artist does not need to understand the jargon of a computer programmer.   It is easy to assume that because a person can speak and read they have all the Word Smarts they need to be able to learn.

### Strategies

Children who are Word Smart may not be school smart. He or she may use their word smart skills inappropriately. Perhaps your child uses her 'word smart' skills to talk in class instead of paying attention, may be a poor reader but a superb storyteller, or enjoy writing poems at home but not doing school assignments.  You may need to talk to your child about when it is appropriate to talking class and when it is not.

## Word Smart Learners and homework

### Explanations

Word Smart learners like things explained to them. Use words to help them understand what they have to do and how they should do it. Do not SHOW your child what to do TELL him or her what to do.

### Self talk

This strategy is used to help children develop foundational learning skills but it is also a good way to help your Word Smart child learn and understand. By listening to you talking your child will understand how to use words, how to make language work for him. Using language in this way helps your child gain information and knowledge. Self talk is explained under 'Show' in the Super Strategies section.

### Opportunities to write

This type of learner likes to write down ideas and thoughts. Writing strategies range from making to-do lists to note taking, from thank you letters to ten page essays. Some Word Smart learners prefer to use spoken rather than written language. These students may need some way to record their thoughts.

### Talking through problems

When your child is struggling to do homework ask him or her to talk about what has to be done and to talk about why there is a problem in doing it. Your child may be able to use his language skills to understand the difficulty and to work out a solution.

### Talk to your child

Talk about your child's feelings and concerns, about what he or she has to do and how it is going to get done. Talk to pass on information. Talk to ask questions. Talk to help your child make sense of the world.

### Listen to your child

Word Smart learners need to use words to help them learn. As they talk to you they are trying to work out their thoughts. You need to listen to what they say so that you can guide their thinking or compliment them on their skills.

Some students can take a few moments to work out what the want to say. Give your child this thinking space and wait quietly until he or she is ready to put thoughts into words.

### Negotiate

This type of learner is very good at using their language skills to get what they want. So, when you want your child to do something try negotiating with them. They will appreciate the chance to try out their skills and you will soon find out who is the best negotiator.

### Jokes

Word Smart people understand jokes. Good jokes can give them new ways of looking at things, of making different types of connections. Just don't expect your child's sense of humor to be the same as yours!

### Knowledge of other ways of learning

Word Smart learners think that all other children learn the same way they do. They expect to be able to talk to someone and be understood. When they learn that other children learn in different ways it helps them communicate with them more easily.

### Words Hurt

Word Smart learners are sensitive to the words they hear. If you have to tell your child that he or she is doing something wrong or that their work is not correct be very careful what you say. Choose your words carefully and start by saying something good before you have to say something bad.

### Say what you mean

Word Smart learners are word sensitive. If you tell your child something and it is not clear what you mean he or she will be confused and you may assume that your child is either not listening or not trying to understand what you say. When speaking to your child about homework or schoolwork try to be as clear as possible. This means thinking about what you are going to say before you say it.

*Mean what you say!*

Word Smart learners will remember what you have said to them. If you have told your child that he can stop work in ten minutes he will remember that and stop working at that time. It is easy to get into 'he said, she said' types of arguments with a Word Smart learner.

*Check the instructions*

Poor instructions, written or spoken, make Word Smart children doubt their own abilities. Some instructions can be very confusing. I have tried to help children complete worksheets with instructions neither of us can understand. It can be really frustrating for a word smart child to be given instructions that are unclear. They find them confusing and do not trust the people who have set them. If your child is given homework and neither of you understand the instructions talk to your child's teacher to get clarification.

*Word Rivers*

This is a good way of getting the words in your child's head onto paper. A child can use this strategy when he or she is not sure what to write or what to say. Ask your child to listen to the words in his or her head and then to write them down – all of them. When all the words are on paper your child can go through them to look for ideas and to start writing.

*Writing book reports*

Writing a good book report after your child has finished reading the whole book can be difficult. Get your child to write one sentence about each chapter that he reads. Then he can put all the sentences together and he has the beginning of a good book report.

*Taking notes*

You can use this strategy for note taking. Get your child to make notes at the end of each chapter or paragraph of his textbook.

# Phrases to use when helping with homework

'Tell me word for word'
'Let's talk about it'
'The word you're looking for is…'
'I hear you but I am not sure that I agree'
'Let me spell it out for you'
'In other words…'

# Word Smart Learners and tutoring

*Type of tutor*

Any tutor who gives verbal instructions and allows and encourages children to express their ideas and feelings will work for this type of learner.

Tutoring situations where students are expected to master material through constant repetition and correction may not be the best approach.

### Type of program

One-on-one or group tutoring will work for this type of learner. If you enroll your child into a group program make sure that the program does not use a step by step repetitive approach to helping children learn. Choose a program where students have a chance to discuss what they are learning.

# Number Smart

## Description

Students who are Number Smart are able to understand systems and patterns, and can rely on abstract thinking to solve problems and make logical and practical decisions more easily than most people.

Number Smart children like order and consistency. They can work with complex sets of rules and procedures but need to understand what they are expected to do. They take a step-by-step approach to getting things done and like to persevere at one task before having to start the next. They are happy working with numbers, they can often solve number puzzles instinctively and can use symbols to represent complex ideas. Some number Smart learners like working with philosophical questions.

The child who continually asks 'why' and who wants to know how things work, and expects you to be able to give reasons for everything, is not trying to annoy you. She is probably Number Smart and this is the way she likes to learn!

## Number Smart Learners and schooling

### Type of school

All schools have a defined structure to the day. Usually classes start at a certain time and last for a certain amount of time and lessons are scheduled at set times during the week. Teachers follow set textbooks and present information in a logical and ordered way. Number Smart students love this approach to teaching because they learn best when work is be presented in an orderly fashion, and in a sequence that makes sense to them. Teachers teach in methodical ways and expect learners to learn in logical steps.

### Strategies

A Number Smart learner fits into the school system well because the way they learn is the way most teachers like to teach. These learners appreciate the step-by-step approach to learning that most teachers use. They follow directions well and are good at explaining how they did their work. They like to progress from easy to more difficult work and are willing to take all the steps they need to be able to do this. Unlike Picture Smart learners they may not be able to 'see' the answers, but they know how to work to get there.

These analytic thinkers like timed tests and can be well organized. They can be good at picking up flaws in arguments that can be annoying to some!

Students who are Number Smart are often thought of as being very intelligent because many standardized tests focus on math skills.

## Number Smart Learners and homework

### Order

This type of learner likes things to be presented in a neat and tidy way, this helps them understand what they are learning. They may not be tidy, but they want their information presented to them in a clear and logical manner. Keep a homework agenda and cross of items when finished. Post homework schedule where it can be seen. Prepare all the materials needed to complete a homework assignment. Have some sequence to actions, such as when one homework assignment is complete put it in the school bag.

### Technology

Because it is logical, does what you tell it, and concerns numbers these learners like to use technology to help solve problems. This includes calculators, computers, and smart phones. Give your child as much access to these technologies as you can.

### Step-by-step approach

Not for them a leap into the unknown, this type of learner wants to know what comes next. They like to see the overall picture before they start something so that they know what they will be expected to do. Setting short-term achievable goals gives them a plan to use. When they are doing homework help them understand what they have to do next to get their work finished.

### Perseverance

All logical thinkers know that if they persevere long enough they will find the answer they are looking for. They can be like a dog with a bone, they will not give up on a problem until they are satisfied that they have done all they can to solve it. Setting time limits for each piece of work will prevent a child not leaving time to finish the next piece of work.

### Strategic thinking

They need to know that there is a strategy that they can follow. They need to know this before they start. Otherwise how are they going to get to where they need to be? You may need to suggest a strategy they could use.

### Logical arguments

They quickly find the logical flaws in arguments, and will only accept those that make sense to them. No getting away with unclear statements with these learners. If you don't feel that you can compete with this way of arguing do not start!

*Use statistics*

If you want to make a point with this type of learner use statistics! They like to make numbers tell them things they need to hear. Use statistics to get your point across. Make sure that you have got them right!

*To-do lists*

This is a good way of creating order out of chaos so that they can do what needs to be done. It is wonderful to cross off completed items.

*Setting priorities*

This is a refinement of the to-do list as it creates a logical order for tasks to be completed. Take the list and write numbers against each activity. Start with number 1.

*Need for speed*

These learners start off as concrete thinkers, the solidity of objects and situations appeals to their logical thinking style. But they soon learn that they can use this thinking style with more abstract things like ideas and analogies. Then they start to soar.

*Need for structure*

Having a structure implies that some logic has been used to create it. These learners understand logic and will search it out. If there is no structure, no logic, they don't know where to begin. They need to know the exact book, page number and section they have to read rather than just being told to read about elephants.

*Clear objectives*

So what exactly are we supposed to do? If a number smart child does not have a clear objective he will not know what steps he needs to take to get here.

## Language to use when helping with homework

'That's logical'
'Follow the process or rules'
'There's a pattern to this'
'Let's make a list'
'We can work it out'
'Prove it!'

## Number Smart Learners and tutoring

*Type of tutor*

This type of learner needs a tutor who has a number smart approach to teaching. The tutor needs to have a defined program for your child, possibly a program that follows what is being taught in school. The tutor should test the child's learning regularly and give the child instructions on how to relearn what he is not sure about. Some type of weekly checklist or progress report would work well with this type of learner.

### Type of program

Number Smart learners benefit from tutoring when they have a specific program to follow, and they know what that program will be, and what the results will be. For that reason some of the proprietary tutoring programs might fit a child who learns this way.

It would be essential to check what the program was offering and to make sure that this matched the needs of your child. A mismatch would lead to your child becoming frustrated and losing confidence in his or her ability to learn.

### Strategies

If you want one-on-one tutoring make sure that the tutor understands your child's need for order and planning and a systematic approach to learning. It would be a good idea set learning goals for each session and ensure that the child understands these.

# Picture Smart

## Description

Students who are Picture Smart possess the ability to visualize the world accurately, modify their surroundings based upon their perceptions, and recreate the aspects of their visual experiences. They are good at remembering images, faces, and fine details and are able to visualize objects from different angles.

Picture Smart learners have great imaginations and can often think of many solutions to a problem. They like being shown what to do rather then being told what to do. They enjoy creating, building and manipulating objects. Picture Smart learners tend to daydream. They are good at visioning – at knowing what the answer will look like – but they struggle to understand the steps they need to take to get there.

Picture Smart learner may be neat or they may not even notice the mess around them.

## Picture Smart Learners and schooling

### Type of school

Picture Smart children may have difficulty learning in school if teachers do not use visual learning resources such as diagrams, mind maps and graphic organizers. Some teachers are very good at using these resources but most teachers rely on words and a logical structure when teaching. This type of learner may benefit by being in a school that is considered less traditional and has a more unstructured approach to teaching and learning.

### Strategies

This type of learner finds it very difficult to take a step-by-step approach to solving problems. They either 'see' the answer or struggle to know how to get to the answer. Teachers may not understand why a bright student cannot always do their work well.

These are the student's whose work is often covered in scribbles and who need to doodle when they are listening to instructions. This may be interpreted as being inattentive and students may get reprimanded when they are only trying to help their brain think.

Picture Smart learners are often late bloomers. Most of the world is set up for Word Smart people and it takes Picture Smart learner a little while to catch up. When they do they can be among the most creative people in the world

## Picture Smart Learners and homework

### Show don't tell

Your child needs you to show him or her what to do. As you are showing your child what to do you can be talking about what you are doing.

### Describe the final result (visioning)

These learners want to know what he final result of their work should look like. Either show them some finished work that looks good or describe what the finished work should look like.

### Help climb the steps

Your child might not know the steps he or she has to take to get their work done. A good way to help is by asking your child what they have to do next and providing answers when they don't know. Writing down the steps and crossing them off when completed is also a good idea.

### Provide pencils and paper

Doodling helps this type of learner think. When children are doodling they are not being inattentive, they are trying to make sense of the information they hear. This type of learner should never be without a pencil and something to doodle on - especially when having to read many words.

### Does that look right?

When helping your child write or spell ask if what they have written looks correct. This type of learner takes note of word shape rather than letter sounds.

### Don't bore them

These learners don't like repetition. Once they know how to do something they want to move on. Getting these learners to practice can be difficult and you need to find a way of making practice fun. Timing their work may help.

### Use diagrams

Diagrams are much easier for a Picture Smart learner to understand than a page of words. Drawing diagrams as you use words to explain things to this type of learner gives them something to look at and something to help them remember.

### Graphic organizers
These are a great way to present different structures for writing and working in a way that is easy to understand and to remember.  Graphic organizers help children translate language into diagrams, making it easier for them to write.

They can be found on the web.

### Put them near a window
Looking at things helps their brains function well.

### Break up text
Large amounts of text can be discouraging. Use highlighters to break up the look of text.

### Visualizations- the pictures they have in their heads
These learners are very good at creating mental images. If your child has difficulty explaining something to you ask him or her to talk about the pictures in their head, this makes explanations much easier for them.

### Good lighting
Check that there is good lighting so your child can see what has to be done.

### Time to visualize
Give these learners time to use their skills of visualization before they start to do their work. This helps them understand what they have to do and how they have to do it.

### Closing their eyes
Sometimes there is too much visual information for this type of learner to process. If your child seems confused ask him or her to close their eyes and concentrate on the pictures in their head. This will help your child sort out his thoughts.

### Look for the pattern
Help your child remember words and tables by pointing out the patterns the letters and numbers make.

### Mind mapping
This is a good way of helping them organize their thoughts. The visual structure of a mind map helps them move from chaos to structure.

### Highlighter and 'Stickies'
These can be used as visual aids to mark important pieces of text or material they want to remember.

*Plenty of spare paper and pens*

This type of learner can never have enough!

## Language to use when helping with homework

'Let's look at it differently'

'See how this works for you'

'I can't quite picture it'

'Let's draw a diagram or map'

'I'd like to get a different perspective'

# Picture Smart Learners and tutoring

*Type of tutor*

These learners really need a tutor who thinks the same way they do, and who uses visual materials to help them learn. It is important that the tutor is also a Picture Smart learner who understands how to adapt 'word' and 'logic' based learning into a visual way of learning.

Remember, MOST teachers (and tutors) are Word Smart and/or Number Smart. Once you find a Picture Smart tutor you will need to hang onto them like gold dust.

*Type of program*

When you hire a tutor, or look into a tutoring service, for your child you need to get samples of the resources they will be using. You need to see materials with diagrams, clear design and structure. If the materials have lots of text and few illustrations, your child will not learn efficiently and you will be wasting your money.

# Nature Smart

## Description

Children who have strong Nature Smarts are nature lovers. They would rather be out in the fields or collecting rocks or flowers than being cooped up in school or at home doing pencil and paper work.

These children like to feel that they are part of things, and if they do not feel they are part of a learning situation they may become uncomfortable and unable to learn. They also like being close to natural things. These children demonstrate a wonderful curiosity about the natural world and they often create collections of rocks, shells and other natural objects. Students who are Nature Smart tend to be well organized and able to pick up on subtle differences in meaning.

# Nature Smart Learners and schooling

## Type of school

Schools do not really cater for students who are Nature Smart. Some schools have started encouraging students to reuse, reduce and recycle and also to give lessons on ecological topics. When I was at school this type of learning was limited to an occasional nature walk and learning about the different types of leaves on trees. Some classes had a small, imprisoned animal that children took it in turns to look after.

If schoolwork has links to nature such as recycling, climate change, saving animal habitat their motivation is likely to soar. Some of these children feel more affiliation with animals that with human beings.

If your child is Nature Smart the world is beginning to open up and need his or her skills.

## Strategies

Sometimes a child's love of nature can be seen as something they can do after they have done their schoolwork. If teachers and parents do not understand their need to incorporate their love of nature into everyday activities these children will feel excluded. In extreme cases this can lead them to perform violent acts as a way of getting noticed.

You may be able to help your child's school start a program that would suit your child. Recycling programs or links to animal welfare agencies would work and arranging for speakers to talk about these issues would always be welcome.

# Nature Smart Learners and homework

It can be difficult to provide situations that promote learning for these children. Homework needs to be done inside and these children thrive outside. There are a few ways you can help.

## Connection to nature

Help your child feel connected to nature by having collections of rocks or leaves near where he works. Some children might find that holding a rock or a playing with a piece of paper will help them concentrate on their work.

## Sit by a window

Sitting by a window allows your child to look outside even if he can't go there.

## Group books

These learners like to put things in groups. You could help by suggesting that your child puts all his workbooks and papers into groups before he starts and then put them in the order he will do the work.

*Mind Maps*

Encourage your child to use Mind Maps. Using these will help your child put his thoughts in order and give a structure to his work.

*Photos of adventures*

Having photos on their workspace of outside adventures they have been on will help them connect to nature.

## Nature Smart Learners and tutoring

*Type of tutor*

If your child needs the services of a tutor you may need to try several different approaches before you find one that fits. These learners benefit most from a tutoring situation where the tutor understands their need for connections with the natural world around them and can relate the work they are doing to this world. Look in Section 3 under Extra support on how to find tutors.

*Type of program*

The type of program that will benefit your child will depend on how People or Self Smart they are. Look at those sections to understand what program your child needs.

In general this type of learner appreciates a less structured approach that allows him or her to use imagination and knowledge of relationships to help learning.

# Music Smart

## Description

People with musical intelligence think in terms of patterns. For example, they look for patterns in new information in order to increase learning. They also look for patterns in speech and language. They remember things by turning them into lyrics or rhymes. People with musical intelligence have a strong appreciation of music and they like to have pleasant sounds to listen to as they learn.

- Like to tap to music and tend to talk themselves through tasks.

- Do not like harsh sounds or random noise.

- Some are deeply spiritual and sensitive to the emotional power of music.

- Like to listen to people talk, especially if they have a pleasing voice and a good presentation style.

- Have the capacity to carry a tune, remember musical melodies, have a good sense of rhythm,

- Enjoy listening to music and may begin moving and singing along.

- Sensitive to nonverbal sounds such as birdsong and traffic noise that others may have missed.

## Music Smart learners and schooling

### Type of school

Music smart learners can thrive in most type of schools. Any school with music based activities such as a choir or a band would be helpful. Few schools incorporate music into regular teaching and this type of learner usually develops their musical abilities in out of school activities.

### Strategies

A child who is predominately Music Smart will prefer to sit in a corner trying to avoid noise. He or she may be tapping on the desk or humming quietly. Do not assume that this child is not listening to what is going on around her, or that her decision to be apart from other children is personal. This child has excellent listening skills but needs to be away from noise so that she can think.

Check whether your school has a band or choir program that your child might like. Volunteer to help with these programs in some way.

Are there musical organizations that would give a presentation to the school?

## Music Smart Learners and homework

### Amount of homework

Music Smart learners who are learning to play an instrument will need time to practice. Too much homework could interfere with them doing this. You may need to talk to your child's teacher if homework gets in the way of music practice.

### Instrument

Have a musical instrument nearby that your child can pick up and play when thinking.

### Background music

Some Music Smart learners like background music while working.

### Lack of stress

This type of learner likes to work in a relaxed situation, try to limit stress and noise.

## Words to use when helping with homework

'I like the sound of that'

'I hear what you are saying'

'Can you see the pattern?'
'Tell it like it is'
'That is music to my ears'

## Music Smart Learners and Tutoring

### Type of tutor

A tutor who understands the student's need for music while learning - perhaps who plays a musical instrument themselves - would be an ideal tutor if they were qualified in the subject the student needs help with.

### Type of program

This type of learner might prefer one-on-one tutoring so he or she has the opportunity to use their musical skills without distracting others.

# Body Smart

## Description

Body Smart Learners think best when they are moving. They need to walk, stretch, feel, and touch to help their brains work. They learn by doing rather than watching or listening and would rather show you how to do something than tell you how to do it.

They respond intuitively to physical stimulus and they learn how to play ball games, ski, dance, quicker and more easily than other types of learners.

They enjoy hands on activities and the company of other physically active children. They communicate through body language and gestures.

## Body Smart Learners and schooling

### Type of school

These learners need a school that gives them many opportunities to move around and to use up their physical energy. They are always going to find being in school difficult. They are the ones who are the first to rush out at recess and to start kicking a ball around. Pent up frustration at being expected to sit still and listen can overflow and they may disrupt the rest of the class by their constant need to be in motion.

### Strategies

The child who finds it hard to sit still in class, who always has something in his hands, who makes faces, and walks around the room is most likely a Body Smart Learner. These learners can drive a teacher crazy. Their constant need for movement does not fit well in a classroom where they are supposed to sit still and listen! Talk to your child about ways he can move around without disrupting the class.

Teachers may not be aware of your child's need to be physically active and may not give your child the opportunity to move around the classroom. This lack of physical activity can cause your child to become frustrated and restless.

Body Smart learners may need to do some physical activity such as running or playing in the park before they are ready to go home.

Ask your child's teacher if your child can hold something while he is listening to her. Give your child something to play with that makes no noise so it doesn't distract other children.

Gym and Sports classes provide welcome breaks for this learner. Encourage your child to join as many of these as possible.

Quiet reading usually means sitting still and this is difficult for this type of learner. Reading is fine, but ask if your child can move around while doing it

## Body Smart Learners and homework

### Walking home
Walking home from school gives your child chance to use up some energy before starting homework.

### Breaks
Body Smart learners need frequent breaks from sitting at a desk or table to do their work. You might use a timer that reminds the child when he can get up and take a five-minute break.

### Space
Give your child space when doing homework so that it is easy for him to get up and move about.

### Walking
Some children think best when they are walking. If your child is struggling to concentrate on work suggest that he walks around the room for a few minutes.

### Music
Let your child listen to music while working. This keeps his brain active.

### Squeeze ball
Playing with a squeeze ball while working may give your child the movement her brain needs.

### Show don't tell
Show your child how to do things rather than telling them what to do and ask them to show you how they do things rather than telling you.

*Energy*

Make sure your child has the energy he needs to do his work. These children can use most of their energy doing sports or games and may have little left for schoolwork. Always keep a snack ready for them.

## Language to use when helping with homework

'Does that feel right to you?'

'Get in touch with…'

'That doesn't sit right with me'

'Do you have a good feeling about this?'

'What is your gut telling you?'

## Body Smart Learners and tutoring

*Type of Tutor*

The tutor should be aware of the child's need to be active and be prepared to modify their teaching methods to take this into account.

Tutoring should take place where there is room for the child to move rather than being restricted to one chair and one desk.

If possible choose a tutor who is also a Body Smart learner. He or she will have a deeper understanding of your child's learning issues and will have developed ways of learning that meet your child's learning needs,

*Type of program*

Body Smart learners may benefit more from one-on-one tutoring than being part of a group. One-on-one tutoring will allow them the freedom to move when they need to without disturbing others.

# Strategies for 'Move to Mastery'

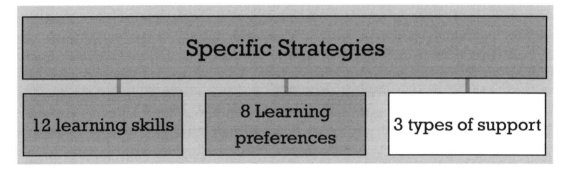

Children need support to **Move to Mastery** when they have to catch up missed or mis-understood lessons, want to accelerate their learning and want new learning opportunities.

> ## Three types of support
> *Catch up*
> *Accelerated learning*
> *New learning opportunities*

You, your child's school, or a tutor, can provide this extra support.

# Catch-up

Children need support this type of support to catch up on a specific subject when they have missed lessons or moved to a school with a different curriculum and to re-learn and understand some of the basic concepts that underlie what they are being taught.

## Catch up missed lessons

*You*

If you intend to deliver the support your child needs to catch up on missed lessons you need to consider the following questions.

- Do I have the time to provide this support?

- Do I have the skills to deliver the content?

- Do I understand the content well enough to teach it?

- Do I know exactly what content my child has missed?

- How am I going to get this information from my child's teacher?

Many parents use tutoring to help children improve their learning ability and get a better understanding of what they are being taught. The problem is tutors may not know what your child's learning needs are and may struggle to understand how to help your child become a better learner. However there is a way to help your child Move to Mastery and develop the skills and strategies they need. It involves you, teachers and tutors working together to provide what your child needs.

You can provide the support that schools and tutors can't. You can help your child learn how to learn and make school make sense. Helping your child in this way will increase your child's ability to learn. The school or tutor can provide the content that will help your child catch up on the learning he or she has not fully understood or learned.

You need to do several things to make this happen. You need to –

- Tell the school and tutor about your child's learning needs and how you are meeting them.

- Provide the school and tutor with strategies that could help your child learn. This is something to discuss with your child's teacher or tutor and negotiate what actions can be taken.

- Develop a good home/school relationship so that communication is quick and easy.

- You will probably be providing support when your child is doing homework. Here are some guidelines for you to consider.

## Homework help

### Your role

Don't do your child's homework. Homework is the responsibility of the student to complete and the teacher to set and mark. Your role is to act as the channel of communication between home and school so that teachers know when homework is too hard or too easy and you know what your child is expected to do.

Tell your child that the homework is his responsibility and that you will help if he asks for help. But you will not do the work for him. You will try to show him what to do and make sure that he understands any instructions.

If your child still has difficulties then you must tell the teacher about them. Teachers rarely get feedback on the type and amount of homework they set and assume that everything is fine unless they are told otherwise. The teacher is only going to be able to help your child if you tell her he needs help.

## Understand expectations

You need to know what expectations your child's teacher has about homework.

- What do teachers expect you to do to help your child?

- How much homework will your child be getting?

- What happens if homework is not completed on time?

- What happen if homework is not completed well enough?

- Will homework marks be part of your child's report cards?

These are good questions to ask at the first meeting you have with your child's teacher.

## The Purpose of homework

Why is your child expected to do homework?  Is it so he can –

- review the work taught in class

- practice what she has been taught

- demonstrate that he knows and understands what has been taught?

- learn new information so he can get through the curriculum?

- learn skills of information gathering?

- express her own ideas and thoughts?

The purpose may change for every assignment. Until you understand the purpose you are limited in the support you can offer. Again, you can discuss this with his teacher.

## Homework schedule

Having a homework schedule help you understand what homework your child has to do and how much time he or she is expected to spend doing it. Not all schools have homework schedules but many do. Once you have a schedule for your child put it where it can be seen and easily referred to. That way there should be no arguments about what homework needs doing, only discussions about changes to the schedule.

## Homework timing

Talk to your child's teacher about how much homework your child should be doing. The general rule of thumb is ten minutes for each grade level. For instance, a child in Grade 1 would have ten minutes doing work he brings home. A child in Grade 12 would have about two hours of homework.

Made in the USA
Charleston, SC
29 December 2016